To Ella
with Love,
from
Xmas. 1922.

D1492325

THE BOOK OF THE CLYDE

BOOKS WRITTEN AND ILLUS-
TRATED BY DONALD MAXWELL

UNKNOWN KENT
UNKNOWN SUSSEX
UNKNOWN SURREY
UNKNOWN ESSEX
UNKNOWN NORFOLK
UNKNOWN SUFFOLK
UNKNOWN DORSET
UNKNOWN SOMERSET
HISTORY WITH A SKETCH-BOOK
A CRUISE ACROSS EUROPE
ADVENTURES WITH A SKETCH-BOOK
THE LAST CRUSADE, 1914–1918
A DWELLER IN MESOPOTAMIA
A PAINTER IN PALESTINE

THE BODLEY HEAD

THE FALLS OF THE CLYDE

THE
BOOK OF THE CLYDE

BEING A CONNECTED SERIES OF
DRAWINGS AND OBSERVATIONS
OF THE RIVER FROM ITS SOURCE
TO THE FIRTH

BY

DONALD MAXWELL

LONDON: JOHN LANE THE BODLEY HEAD LIMITED

First Published in 1927

MADE AND PRINTED IN GREAT BRITAIN
BY JARROLD AND SONS LTD. NORWICH

CONTENTS

LIST OF ILLUSTRATIONS

THE BOOK OF THE CLYDE

LIST OF ILLUSTRATIONS

THE RETURN OF THE NATIVE

IT has long been to me a source of reproach among my numerous Scottish friends that I have written so voluminously of places upon the earth, but not of Scotland.

It has been an affront—so one man tells me—that I speak of myself as a Man of Kent and write books in a humorous vein for the benefit of the denizens of the Garden of England, no doubt assuming that north of the Tweed there is no man who can see a joke. Recently a northern patriot met

1

me in the Strand, bore me off in triumph to lunch with him at the Caledonian Club, and attacked me on the subject of the neglect of my native heath.

The upshot of it all was that I started for Scotland within the week. I booked to Thornhill, that being the nearest convenient centre for Maxwelton Braes.

The charges against me were mostly true. The long residence of my immediate forefathers in the South had dimmed that much-to-be-envied local patriotism. My father was born in Kent and thus I am indeed a Man of Kent, apart from a long " qualification " acquired by having lived in the county for many years. I fear, too, it is a fact that I have regarded Scotland as a friendly but foreign country—a Christian country, it is true, but over-shadowed by strange Protestant superstition. My mother lived in Scotland when a girl and I remember as a small boy being terribly and crushingly impressed by her vivid account of a certain Scottish Sunday. It was in Glasgow and she and her sister were trying over some hymn tunes on the piano, with a view to taking a Sunday school class, when a solemn knock upon the front door caused the harmless rehearsal to cease. A policeman had come to remind them that it was the Sabbath. A further depression was made upon my young mind on being told that in Scotland the great and joyous festival of Christmas was not observed, that shops were open upon that Holy Day and business transacted as usual. I was only a child at the time I heard

A FARM IN DUMFRIESSHIRE

THE EASTERN BORDERS OF ENGLAND AND SCOTLAND

these things, but for many years afterwards I found myself confusing the Scotch with the Jews.

All my southern prejudices concerning the Scottish character were overturned at once as I crossed the border at Gretna. Putting to the test the theory that the Scot lacks humour, I tried my best joke on the railway porter at the station and he roared with laughter. At the same time I bought a magazine and had not sufficient change. A fellow-traveller, obviously a Scot, *insisted on lending me sixpence* !

5

MAXWELTON HOUSE

In a subsequent conversation I found that I had become a Nonconformist. This intelligence surprised me. After being a churchwarden for fifteen years (I speak as a fool) and a pillar of episcopacy, I found myself possessed of the Nonconformist conscience. That was too much!

So I start—as far as Scottish things are concerned—as a complete agnostic. I will begin to trace the Clyde from its source to its mouth and pick up whatsoever I can of Scottish ways and Scottish scenes and learn, too, of Scottish history by the banks of her most famous river. I will scribble my own maps and choose my own impressions and if any stranger care to come with me on this pilgrimage I will be to him a cheerful guide.

From the heights of Maxwelton Braes I could see the rolling range of the Lowther Hills spread out to the north-east, Queensberry overtopping the rest,

THE CLYDE NEAR ELVANFOOT

at the height of 2,285 feet. It is from these bare uplands that the Daer Water and the Portrail Water rise, to meet near Elvanfoot where the small brook traditionally known as the Clyde (though one of its shortest sources) joins them.

I can sketch here a view of Maxwelton House in which lived Annie Laurie, famous in song, but I cannot give you any explanation, scientific or otherwise, as to why the dew should fall earlier on this heathy tract than in other parts of Scotland.

The exact spot at which the Clyde rises is a matter of pious opinion. If you will look at the rough sketch-map on page 14 you will see that the biggest branches reach up to the hills by Queensberry and that the Daer Water is actually the longer of the two chief streams.

There is a wonderful way over the Dalveen Pass which brings the traveller to the Portrail Water and

lower down to the point where the Daer Water joins
it, at a spot just above Elvanfoot, a very small
stream which rises in the steeps of Clyde Law and
runs into the Daer Water. This, for some reason
difficult to determine, is reckoned as the one only
and true source of the Clyde.

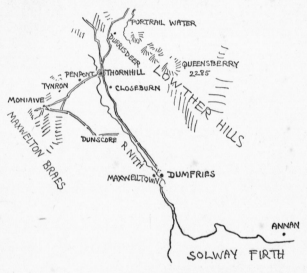

MAXWELTON BRAES AND THE LOWTHER HILLS

At Durisdeer is an old track, said to be a Roman
road, making a shorter route than the pass, but it is
rough and inadvisable for motorists. It comes out
alongside Portrail Water before it joins the present
road and is merged with it.

I am quite a novice at place-names and love to
hazard guesses as to the origin of words. I suspect

that Daer Water has nothing to do with deer, but must be the Celtic *dwr*. The same river name occurs in Kent, the Dour which gives Dover its name, the Douro in Portugal, the Adur in Sussex, the Durbeck in Nottinghamshire, the Dour also in Fife and Aberdeen, and countless other combinations. Probably Stour, so common in England, is

NEAR THE DALVEEN PASS

a conglomerate word formed by *uisge*, water, and *dwr* also water. (Esk, Axe, Usk, Wisk and other river names are derived from this root). It is interesting to note that whisky and water are derived from the same source. That is no doubt why they go so well together. In the case of Daer Water, there is an obvious redundancy, very common in place names, both words meaning the same thing, as in Brendon Hill (Somerset) which is a threefold redundancy—*bryn*, *don* and *hill*.

9

As to the meaning of Portrail I am baffled altogether. Perhaps some Scottish reader will enlighten me. The name Clyde is evidently derived from the Gaelic *clith*, strong. Probably the Cludan in Scotland, the Clwyd, the Cloyd and the Clydach in Wales, and the Glyde in Ireland are names derived from the same word.

LITTLE CLYDE FARM

THE popular and orthodox source of the Clyde is taken to be the one that rises about two miles from Elvanfoot. I sought it out, and was directed to a group of buildings known as Little Clyde Farm. These stand at the foot of Clyde Law, the hill from which, according to an ancient couplet, two other rivers of Scotland have their origin.

> Annan, Tweed and Clyde
> Rise a' out o' ae hill-side.

The second line will want a bit of unravelling by Men of Kent and other uninstructed southerners,

2   II

but roughly I suppose it to mean : " Rise all out of the same hill-side."

The way to Little Clyde Farm is along the road to Carlisle. Over the bridge at Elvanfoot I was directed to the point where the road crosses the railway. There is a gate to the left, just before the railway bridge. This leads to a cottage and further on to the Farm. As it is all private land I sought permission from Mr. Thompson (and was readily granted the same) to track the tiny stream as far as I could to find the actual spring.

At first I thought the Clyde undoubtedly emerged from barrels, and I could see no other fount (p. 16). Perhaps my etymological guess was right, whisky and Clyde water having strange relationship from the very first. Soon, however, I discovered my mistake.

The burn that fed this pool was hidden and this place of barrels was no doubt used as a cooper's accessory. The barrels and tubs were put there to swell after getting too dry.

Above this place I went some few hundred feet. There were little houses, proving on closer inspection to be chicken runs, and through a sunny cleft in the hillside poured the infant Clyde in miniature waterfalls (page 13).

The place where the Daer Water and the Portrail Water meet and the winding portion of the river below this forms an involved pattern of loops, and when seen at twilight, as I have sketched it on page 17, looks like a silver snake creeping through the dark vale. At the bridge at Elvanfoot we can call the river the Clyde without fear of controversy. Tributaries rapidly swell its volume. The Elvan Water comes in on the left, and before we reach

"THE SOURCE OF THE CLYDE"

Crawford the Midlock Water and the Camps Water have added their tribute.

We must remember that this part of the Clyde valley carried one of the Roman roads to the north, and in view of this fact I cannot help being immensely interested in some of the place-names. We have seen that there is a Roman track—the Well Path—from Durisdeer over the region of the Dalveen Pass and at Beattock we are on that Roman road that goes north from Carlisle. I have little archæological knowledge and throw this out as a mere guess. Does the name Camps Water tell us anything of a Roman station ? Does Rome Hill— a curious designation among Celtic place names— indicate anything ? A little farther on at Moat Farm about three miles below Abington we shall come across great earthworks. Were these anything

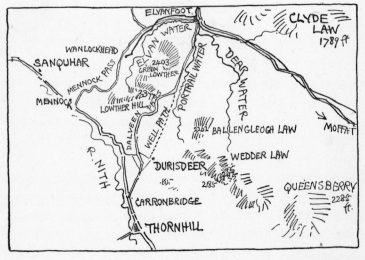

THREE SOURCES OF THE CLYDE

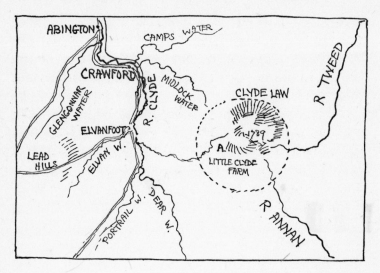

THE SOURCE OF THREE RIVERS

to do with Roman occupation? I know many of those earthworks are pre-Roman, but especially in regions where the hills determine the choice of the position of a road, it is common to find the Romans improving on existing communications rather than cutting new ones.

There are few roads, if any, in Scotland that were made by the Romans as purely military ways for marching men and travelling dead straight over hill and dale as they do in the south. For one thing the rugged nature of the country makes straight going almost impossible.

Rome had not the same motive in ruling Scotland

as in ruling England. Her chief intention was to keep those troublesome people from the North from coming down and raiding the South; hence the great walls which she built as a safeguard against surprise.

The name of Camps Water, I find on inquiry, is probably called so because the burn runs by a place that may have been a camp. Whether this was a Roman Camp or not does not matter. If this was thought to be a camp, even erroneously, it would account for the name.

THE LOOPING RIVER NEAR ELVANFOOT

THE GROWING RIVER

CRAWFORD is a straggling place with little to detain us in its street ; but a few hundred yards below, the valley lies spread out beneath the steep slopes of Drake Law on the West. A farm appears, dwarfed by the bare green flanks of the valley and possessing little woodland amenities which give a graciousness to a rather bare landscape. I have sketched this scene on page 23. A few hundred yards farther down the valley and looking back the other way, we see Crawford and a glittering loop of the now wide-spreading shallow expanses of the young Clyde, and a glimpse of Tower Lindsay.

17

This latter ruin is that of a stronghold once defended by a moat. It was, as its name indicates, the seat of the Lindsays, afterwards Earls of Crawford, from the close of the twelfth century till 1488. In the reign of William the Lion, the barony of Crawford Lindsay was held in lordship of " Sweyne, son of Thor," names which show a former Norse occupation of this part.

Taking part with the unlucky James III in his quarrel with the nobles, the estates of the Crawfords were forfeited and granted to Archibald " Bell-the-Cat " Earl of Angus.

Before Abington is reached we come to a turning on the left. This is a by-road that leads back in a southerly or south-westerly direction following the Glengonnar Water (along its western bank) till it comes to Smelting Mill. The name tells us that we are at the foot of the Leadhills. The fastnesses of this region and further on Wanlockhead and the solemn and wild Mennock Pass are full of dramatic " memories " of the hunted and persecuted Covenanters. A hundred stories will be told you gladly by the people of these hills. I listen with interest and not a little awe at the tremendous impression those days of strife have left upon the minds of the descendants of these persecuted people.

It would seem a pity to spoil the picture by any sort of scepticism. No doubt hundreds of harmless folk were literally martyrs for the faith that was in them, but I cannot help remembering that there were also among them unscrupulous and

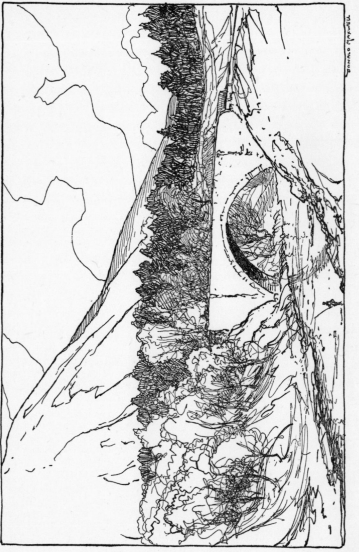

ELVANFOOT

bloodthirsty fanatics who would have stopped at nothing had they got the upper hand.

Perhaps I am wrong, but it is from a source north of the Tweed that I have acquired a certain hesitation in accepting everything that these brave men

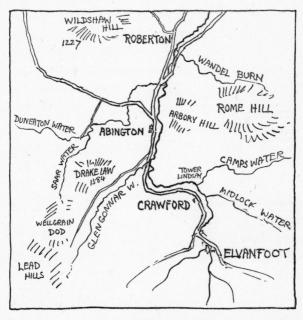

FROM ELVANFOOT TO ROBERTON

did, as being for the liberty of conscience. The acid test of your toleration is your willingness to welcome toleration for others when you have unlimited political power. Was Scott too fanciful in his picture of these times? Are the pages of *Old*

Mortality to be trusted as reasonably true to history or does the great romancer colour up the picture too much, for the sake of contrast ?

Retracing our steps and joining the main road again just above Abington we find the view which I have tried to depict on page 31. It is from here that we come to a stretch of the river, beyond which appears the great conical peak—Tinto—the Hill of Fire, so called, some have said, because of the heathen fires of ancient Caledonian worship upon its summit. It may have been one of the " high places " of the days of Druid sacrifices.

Since then, whatever the origin of the name, such a height must have been used again and again as a beacon hill. We shall see it better soon, but as it will dominate the landscape for many miles, we will discuss it now.

It rises at the meeting of the parishes of Carmichael, Wiston, Symington, and Covington. Standing alone and dominating the hills like a monarch among his nobles, it is the loftiest of the southern heights of the central lowlands. Its base is some fifteen miles in circumference. On its south-east side is the site of an ancient castle rejoicing in the name of Fat Lips. Upon its summit is a cairn. It is recorded that a form of penance in old days was to carry a stone to the top of Tinto. The custom is still maintained by tourists, doing it for fun ! Comment on the extraordinariness of human nature is superfluous. When one man does for amusement what another does for punishment, the

A FARM NEAR CRAWFORD

conclusion is that compulsion is what rankles most
in human affairs.

This historic hill, whether because of its myths
or because of its curious and noticeable shape, I
know not, figures in many old-world rhymes such
as Dr. John Brown's *Jeems the Door Keeper* :

> On the Tintock top there is a mist
> And in that mist there is a kist.

At Abington there will be time to take the turning
to the left, and, after some seven or eight miles,
make the acquaintance of the romantic Douglas
Water and see the Douglas Castle. This is the
original of Castle Dangerous of Scott's novel, but
all that remains of the original building described
by the novelist is a single tower surrounded by ash-
trees.

The legend on which Scott builds his story is
that which tells of a beautiful English girl, Lady
Augusta de Berkeley, who in answer to her numerous
suitors offered to wed the knight who should hold
Castle Dangerous for a year and a day.

The gage was almost won by brave Sir John de
Walton, when Douglas, who had landed with Bruce
at Turnberry on his return from exile, sent Sir John
defiance that, notwithstanding his vigilance and
valour, he would be in possession of his own Castle
of Douglas by the following Palm Sunday.

On the day named, Douglas collected his retainers,
and with the aid of an old servant of the family fell

upon the English garrison as they returned from church, and having overpowered them, took the castle. Sir John de Walton was killed in the fight.

Abington makes a good centre for the exploration of this part of the Clyde valley. It is the first place we come to on the river where the hills are well wooded. Hitherto, the great hills, impressive as they are, seem in some lights to be rather austere and overpowering. Here a belt of woodland hangs from hill to hill and the glittering waters wending their way beneath its shade give a new note to the scenery.

A little beyond the village and on the banks of the stream is a delightful prospect as the traveller looks back towards Crawford. I have endeavoured to record some shadow of this on page 37. The bridge, which is not in itself either striking or beautiful, as seen from here makes a delicate link between the two masses of trees on either hand. The great and impressive slope that lifts itself above the river on the left is at its lower extremity named Arbory Hill. It leads on to the greater height of Rome Hill, the name of which we have noted before. This massive bastion divides Camps Water from the Wandel Burn which joins the Clyde two miles lower down.

Again our interest in river names is aroused. Is this word a relative of our old friend the Wandel of South-west London? I am only a guesser at these things. The Celtic *avon* " a river " gives, among many others, the names Oundle (Avondale), Wandle and Wandsworth.

BETWEEN ABINGTON AND CRAWFORD

TOWER LINDSAY

BY TOWER LINDSAY

TOWER LINDSAY, very often referred to as
Crawford Castle, is so hidden away by trees
that it would be quite easy to miss it altogether.
Very little of it remains, for, like all these ruins,
it has no doubt served as the local quarry in times
gone by for the building of farm-houses and walls.
In England Henry VIII often has to bear the
brunt of vandalistic infamy which was not always
his but the spoliation of succeeding generations.
The romantic movement of the early nineteenth

29

century and the Gothic revival period did a great deal to arrest this habit of stone robbery. For the first time people began to see the value of preserving these landmarks of history.

The eighteenth century was the worst sinner, artistically, for it destroyed ruthlessly much of the work that remained of ancient abbeys and castle towers. It had not the excuse (bad as the excuse was) either of greed or fanaticism. It did not object to ruins in the abstract. So depraved was its taste that it frequently pulled down the old ruins and *built new ones*—complete with broken arches, time-worn steps and ruined battlements ! An example of this can be seen at Gunnersbury Park where a neat ruined chapel in Gothic style *and in yellow brick* replaces a genuine mediæval relic. Muddleheadedness of intention and meanness of execution could go no farther.

I do not know whether these ruins in the valley of the Clyde are in various private hands or kept as national monuments, but I have a quarrel with some person or persons unknown as to their environment. It is an old saying that sometimes you cannot see the wood for the trees. It is certainly true that many views and many ruins are spoilt by trees. Bothwell Castle from Blantyre Priory is wellnigh invisible, except in fragmentary glimpses from time to time between branches. Lamington Tower is set in a dense screen. Corra Linn would be far more impressive if you could see it from various points of view at present blotted out and

DISTANT TINTO : A VIEW NEAR ABINGTON

rendered "blind" by foliage. The picturesque castle at the top is almost invisible.

Lindsay Tower is no exception. It stands so mixed up with trees that its outline is only apparent in the winter. It would be a great gain, when there are so many trees, to open out vistas and thus get

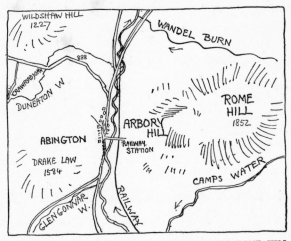

ABINGTON AND ROME HILL

effective views of these old walls against a background of foliage.

The mound on which the remains of Tower Lindsay stand probably dates from the days before the Romans came this way. The name of Crawford is sufficient to tell of its strategic importance. Wherever there is a ford in a pass or narrow valley there must always have been a strong inducement for maintaining a fort.

33

There was a castle here, a place of some strength, in the days of Edward I and it was held by an English garrison when William Wallace captured it. The story goes that most of the English soldiers had crossed the ford to the place where the village now stands and were making merry at the inn, when the small Scottish force descended on the castle and, finding it but lightly defended, took it with ease.

This castle was enlarged and strengthened, but does not figure prominently in Scottish history until it became a Royal Palace for King James V about 1530 until his death in 1542. The architectural "reformation" and change from a grim fortress to a stately palace is attributed to Sir James Hamilton of Finnart, the King's architect. His work remains at Linlithgow and Holyrood, but there is nothing now here save a few stones to reveal the family likeness in architecture.

In Mr. MacCullum Scott's recent work on Clydesdale in the chapter called "The King's Hunting" there is an instructive note on the architecture of this ruin which is well worth looking up. Speaking of the first castle at the time of Wallace he writes :

"At some later period the wing on the south has been added, and this is now the best preserved fragment. . . . The main building has been remodelled in some age of greater security, when the stern necessities of defence had given place to culture and refinement. . . . Still later there would seem to have been another change. The interval of security and growing culture has passed away, and the fear of war returned. The beautiful windows are now a source of danger. They have been walled up with rubble stone. In one case, where the stones have broken away, the original iron bars with which the window was grated may still be seen embedded in the stonework which has been built into the window."

This can all be seen to-day. Mr. MacCullum Scott should have been a detective.

The " Good Sir James " is the most romantic figure bound up with the stories of this valley, this gallant knight who essayed to carry the heart of Bruce to the Holy Land and thus fulfil the Scottish King's last wish.

> Thou knowest the words King Robert spoke
> Upon his dying day,
> How he bade me take his noble heart
> And carry it far away.

> And lay it in the holy sod
> Where once the Saviour trod,
> Since he might not bear the blessed cross
> Nor strike one blow for God.[1]

We read in the Chronicles of Scotland that " Quhen Schir James Douglas was chosin as maist worthy of all Scotland to pass with King Robert's hart to the Holy Land, he put it in ane cais of gold, with aromitike and precious unyementies . . . he buryit the said hart, with maist reverence and solempnitie that could be devisit."

[1] *Lays of the Scottish Cavaliers* (W. E. Aytoun).

35

This last statement is considered by historians to be a pious invention. The facts of the case were that good Sir James sailed with Sir Simon of Lee and other knights ; but that on the way they landed in Spain to help the King of Leon and Castile against the Moors. In a fight in which he bore himself most gallantly Sir James was killed in trying to succour one of his knights who was hard pressed by the infidels. Thus fell Black Douglas, one of the band of heroes in the great struggle for Scottish independence waged by Bruce and Wallace. The small company sailed back to Scotland.

No welcome greeted our return,
  Nor clang of martial tread,
But all were dumb and hushed as death
  Before the mighty dead.

We laid our chief in Douglas Kirk
  The heart in fair Melrose ;
And woeful men were we that day—
  God grant their souls repose.

AT ABINGTON

GREEN MYSTERIES

THERE is always a particular fascination in contemplating ancient remains, such as Stonehenge or Old Sarum, because there is a strong element of mere speculation in dogmatizing about them. I think there is something attractive in being able to advance a theory which no one can definitely or with any degree of certainty disprove. I can hold that Stonehenge was a prehistoric clock to tell the times and seasons for planting and sowing.

39

You, on the other hand, can demonstrate that it was constructed solely to symbolize the Sun Worship of the ancients. Another may prove to his entire satisfaction that it is the final and unanswerable demonstration of the fact that we are the Ten Lost Tribes of Israel.

There is not half as much fun in arguing about mediæval architecture. If Jones explains to his lady friends that the flying buttresses of Westminster Abbey were built by Alfred the Great when he threw out a wing at the Restoration, some one is sure to put a spoke in his wheel and demonstrate clearly that he is wrong. But Robinson can tell his best girl that the arches at Stonehenge were devised by the Druids as sheltered spots for growing mistletoe, thus making kissing a religious duty. No one can throw cold water on his theory and he may be able to get away with it.

This upper region of the Clyde Valley is particularly rich in old camps and mounds. The site of Tower Lindsay is we have seen, probably, very old and the Norman and mediæval work was the adaptation of an existing earth fortress. The top of Arbory Hill opposite Abington, is marked in an old map of Ross's in 1773, as a " Druid Temple."

Further down the stream there is a curious and striking grass mound and on it is a group of buildings known as Moat Farm. There is a mill there and a small pond some fifty feet above the river. A superficial observer would see in this the *moat*. A little thought, however, will evolve a theory that this

MOAT FARM

DONALD MAXWELL

spelling of *moat* has been the cause of confusion. It should evidently be *mote*, and this miniature Mt. Sinai was once the place for the proclaiming of laws and the council or parliament of a thousand years ago.

Hear Isaac Taylor: " In Scotland the ancient place of assembly was the Mote Hill at Scone, near the ancient capital of Scotland. In the midst of the town of Hawick there is a singular conical mound called the Moat Hill. We may also notice the names of the Moot Hill at the eastern end of Lyne Bridge, and the Mote of the Mark in Galloway. On the confines of the Lake District there are hills called Montay and Caermote ; and there is Moot-Hill at Naseby, all of which have probably served as the meeting places of assemblies."

As I have said, I am only a guesser and merely show you by means of sketches what these places are like and leave you to go on guessing—perhaps offering a few unmethodical and unscientific hints. But if you would go a step further in unravelling these mysteries take with you Mr. A. MacCullum Scott's delightful book *Clydesdale,* a book to which I have already drawn your attention. I have only just run across it since I returned with my notes and drawings, and I only wish I had been able to take it with me when exploring. Here is a note about Arbory Hill :

" . . . one day I chanced to look down from Tewsgill, which rises behind it 450 feet higher. I stared in amazement. The dome of Arbory was fortified by three concentric arcs of massive walls which lay mapped out beneath me with all the sharpness and precision of a relief model. The Ordnance Survey map had indicated an 'Earthwork' here, but I was not prepared for a Colosseum.

" On closer inspection my amazement increased. This prehistoric fortification is a stupendous work. It measures about 400 feet across, from outer edge to outer edge. The two outer walls, or ramparts, are of earth and stone about 6 feet high. The inner circle is of stone, unhewn, uncemented, and piled together in confusion without any indication of having ever been built into a wall. . . . It is the most remarkable prehistoric monument in Clydesdale, and there are few to equal it in Scotland."

It is evident that whenever it was built the object was to make a sort of Gibraltar of it—a fortress that would hold the pass. Perhaps the name of Abington may throw some light on to this green mystery.

The successive waves of military conquest must have passed up the Clyde valley. The Roman roads and camps are probably only adaptations of what was there before and not as in England new communications deliberately built for the marching of troops. The Romans no doubt held these places against the hostile Celts. When, however, the legions withdrew, these ways and hill forts would have been manned against the Saxon invaders by the British forces. The advancing Saxon would have done just as the Romans had done, secured the passes and strongly guarded their communications.

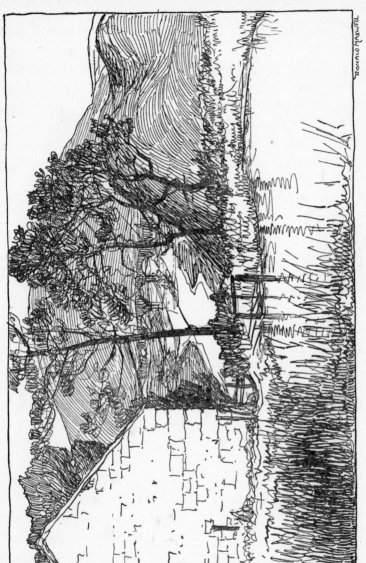

THE POND AT MOAT FARM

RONALD MAXWELL

You will observe on the map a wedge of Saxon place-names driven into the Celtic place-names. Crawford, Abington, Robertson, Lamington, Weston, Symington—all are Saxon, but the hills and more distant places keep their old Celtic nomenclature.

Now it would be no use marching through Clydesdale to subdue it and then going away again. A remnant of half-defeated people could hide and rally once more. The later history of the persecuted Covenanters demonstrated that possibility as far as hiding was concerned. The only way to conquer Clydesdale would be to keep it in continuous occupation.

Now we know from analogy that Saxon names with *ing* in them are generally permanent family settlements. The patronymic of the *Ælings* made *Allington* in Devon, Dorset, Hants, Kent, Wilts and Lincolnshire as well as *Alencthum* in Artois and *Alaincourt* in Lorraine. [For it seems that settlements of these Saxon families were made in other parts of Europe than England.]

In like manner the family name *Æbings* appears in *Aubigny* and *Epinac* (Burgundy), at *Abingdon* (Berkshire), and at *Abington* (Cambridgeshire). It is therefore reasonable to assume that this enterprising family sent out a branch to settle in Clydesdale and this fortified hill was the protection of the Abing *ton*.

About two miles below Abington, on the way to Lanark, the road passes Moat Farm, and if the traveller will look over the low wall to his right he will see more or less the view I have sketched on page 45. In the foreground is the little mill-pond. Far down below is the Clyde and a glimpse of the Bridge that carries the road to Biggar, and on the right is the miniature mountain of the Mote.

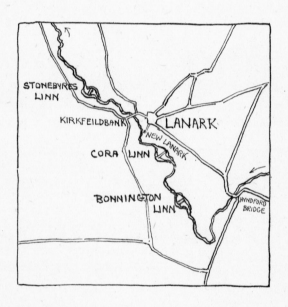

A BASTION OF TINTO

AT THE FOOT OF TINTO

THE "Statistical Survey of Scotland" of 1840 is not half so dull as its title would suggest it to be. In fact the only really dull thing about it is its title. Somewhere amongst its fifteen mighty volumes is an account of the origin of Windgate House near Lamington.

"In the wild but beautifully romantic glen of Keygill, near the head of the stream and at the very base of a steep and lofty hill named Windgill Bank, stand the ruins of Windgate House. This house

49

was built at a remote period by the laird of Lammingtoune at a time when a feud existed between him
and the laird of Symington.

" The latter had erected a building on the side of
Tinto, called Fatlips Castle, which, being directly
opposite, completely overlooked by its elevated
situation, the castle of Lammingtoune, the residence
of his rival laird. It is recorded that he sent a
taunting message to Lammingtoune in no very
delicate terms, to the effect that his wife could not
go out of doors but her motions might be observed
from Fatlips ; which so incensed the chief of the
Baillies that he vowed that, ere that day twelve-
month, he would have a house for himself and his
family, where his wife's motions could neither be
watched by Symington or any one else, and where,
on looking out, he should be able to call everything
that he saw his own. The result was the building
of a residence in Keygill Glen, about four miles from
the village and in the very wildest and most remote
outskirts of the estate of Lammingtoune."

This residence is still to be found by explorers.
It lies hidden in a lonely valley known as Keygill or
Cowgill. There is a small lake up there and as
wild a piece of country as you will find anywhere.
Near it is a strange ruin. There are vaults and
some traces of a stronghold. Local tradition of course
attributes it all to Wallace, but there seems to be
no evidence at all as to its history beyond such
deductions as can be made by observation and
intelligent reconstruction.

DONALD MAXWELL

WALLACE'S TOWER

Of course, our archæological detective—Mr. MacCullum Scott—has been there. He does not miss much. He sees in it more than a place designed to resist a casual raid of cattle lifters. " So elaborate a concealment, so formidable a defence seem rather to belong to the times of the Wars of Independence. When the tide of English invasion rolled over Strathclyde, when the strong castles of Douglas and Bothwell were in the possession of the enemy, when small fortresses like Lamington Tower in the line of the main stream of invasion could not hope to hold out, Windgate Hall may well have been the burrow in which the Lairds of Lamington went to earth."

Lamington Tower, which I have sketched on page 51, is popularly supposed to date from the days of Wallace, whose wife, Marion Bradfute, is said to have been born here. Very little is left of it and even that little is most effectively masked with trees. A fragment of the lofty north-west angle of the structure is all that remains and much of that is not earlier than the sixteenth century. However, this is undoubtedly the site of the building around which so much romance has clung. I had the utmost difficulty in obtaining this view. From the Lamington side of the river, the artist is too near to get anything but a rather uninteresting mass of trees with a small fragment of masonry sticking out of them.

From the other side of the river, however, there would I knew be an effective view, but the problem was how to get there. It is easy to be wise after the event. I ought to have gone to the station and obtained permission to walk down the railway line. However, I succeeded after many adventures in reaching the point from which I made the sketch. From the road on the Symington side is a long trek over an immense field. When I had crossed that I found a stream too wide to jump and too formidable to wade. At last I came to a fence with a bar hung across the water. The wretched thing swung backwards and forwards as I crawled, and, had I not been pretty hardened to climbing, I should have certainly been precipitated into the rushing water.

The Rubicon had been crossed, but an apparently endless waste of sedge and waterlogged country made progress very difficult, and then, when I thought it was all over, I had to make a detour around a vast crop of green corn. Such strength as I had left at the end of all this I put into the drawing. It was very hot and a distant thunderstorm was raging in the direction of Glasgow. Afterwards I found that half the city had been flooded and they had experienced a storm of unusual severity, so I had been well out of it.

The more recent history of Lamington is the history of the Lord Lamington who, as a young man of twenty, inherited the estate—just ninety-one years ago. He found a ruin and a tribe of "aborigines." He left (at his death in 1890) a model village, a happy tenantry and, most wonderful of all in this *via dolorosa* of the martyrs of the

TINTO, FROM NEAR LAMINGTON

DONALD MAXWELL

Covenant, an Episcopal church, and withal a name that will be beloved for many a long day.

The Clyde below Lamington sweeps on in a north-easterly direction and approaches within two miles of Biggar, and would appear to be making for the valley of the Tweed when it suddenly thinks better of it and doubles back to Thankerton.

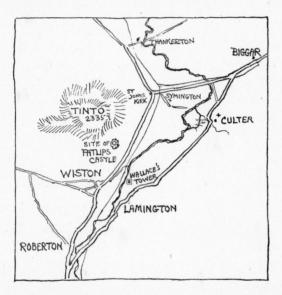

In this neighbourhood tradition asserts that there was a great victory won by Wallace, who had been encamped on the slopes of Tinto. Before the fight he had entered the enemy's camp disguised as a cadger (a seller of provisions), and in this manner found out all about their strength and position. He was, however, suspected and followed, and when he came to a bridge over the Biggar Water at the end of the town he was compelled to turn on his pursuers. The foremost of these was killed and the " cadger " escaped. The bridge is still known as Cadger's Bridge.

Gladstone's ancestors came from Biggar, and there is a story told about Gladstone causing great offence to the elders of the kirk by referring to the architecture of the old collegiate church as being in the style of " debased Gothic." In vain did the minister explain that this was only an art expression and meant no insult. " Well, well," exclaimed one of the dissatisfied elders, " airt or no airt, Meester Gladstone should have written aboot the auld kirk in a ceevil manner."

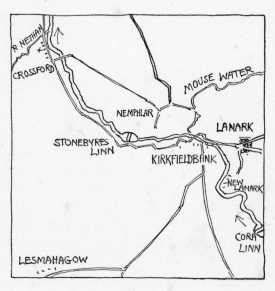

ABOVE THE FALLS

THE road from Lamington to Biggar runs through the village of Culter. A branch road to the left comes out on to the Biggar-Lanark road at the bridge, or rather the bridges, for there are several, by Culter station. The drawing on page 61 was made from the river bank just above this point. The sketch at the top of this page, however, is the view the traveller obtains from the bridge and is looking upstream. The towers of Stenhouse appear " bossom'd high in tufted trees," and the view is a delightful one.

A road to Thankerton runs along the north bank

of the river, but the main road is the one that crosses the bridge in a westerly direction. The first view of the river and bridge below Thankerton is a very striking one. The bridge, an old structure, is seen picturesquely at the bend of the river. Beyond it and below it the river loops and loops through the green land and fulfils somewhat the Tennysonian vision of :

> A full fed river winding slow,
>   By herds upon an endless plain
> The ragged rims of thunder brooding low,
>   With shadow streaks of rain.

In Thankerton there are some beautiful old cottages, thatched and in the true country style, not imitating the worst architectural features of the Cromwell Road in Kensington as so many Scottish villages delight to do—at least that is how it strikes me as an artist.

We have been speculating about place-names, and Thankerton has a familiar sound to a Man of Kent. There is a place just east of Whitstable named Tankerton. I am frankly suspicious about the H. Here is a quotation bearing on the subject. It is from Isaac Taylor's great classic, *Words and Places :*

"There are some curious memorials of that influx of Anglo-Norman nobles into Scotland which took place during the reigns of David I and Malcolm Canmore. In ancient records the name of Maxwell

BRIDGE NEAR SYMINGTON

BRIDGE AT THANKERTON

is written in the Norman form of Maccusville, the
name of Robert de Montealt has been corrupted into
Mowatt and Moffat ; and the families of Sinclair,
Fraser, Baliol, Bruce, Campbell, Colville, Somerville,
Grant (le Grand), and Fleming, are all, as their
names bear witness, of Continental ancestry. Richard
Waleys—that is Richard the Foreigner—was the
ancestor of the great Wallace, and has left his name
at Richardtun in Ayrshire. The ancestor of the
Maule family has left his name in Maleville, or
Melville, in Lothian. Seton takes its name from a
Norman adventurer called Say, *Tankerton in Clydes-
dale, was the fief of Tancard, or Tancred, a Fleming
who came to Scotland in the reign of Malcolm IV."*

The Clyde is now flowing upon a more level region
of ground. It winds and winds and runs more
gently. This is only the calm before the storm, for
soon it plunges down and appears at a level some
three hundred feet below this plateau. The three
falls of the Clyde (Bonnington, Corra, and Stonebyres)

account for over two hundred feet and there are rapids and steep descents between these points.

The country-side as we approach the first great fall, where near Bonnington the river is lost among densely wooded heights, is pleasant and smiling. Campbell sings of this :

> It was a sweet and autumn day
> As ever shone on Clyde
> And Lanark's orchards all the way
> Put forth their golden pride.

I tremble to think what Campbell would have written concerning the shrinking up of the falls of Clyde by means of electric power stations.

> And they call this Improvement ? to have changed
> My native Clyde, thy once romantic shore
> Where Nature's face is banished and estranged
> And Heaven reflected in thy native wave no more ;
> Whose banks, that sweetened May-day breath before
> Lies sere and leafless now in summer's beam
> With sooty exhalations cover'd o'er
> And for the daisied green-sward down thy stream
> Unsightly brick-lanes smoke and clanging engines gleam.

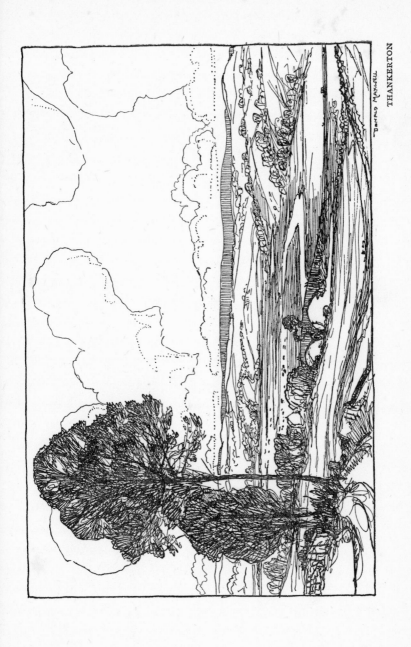

THANKERTON

DONALD MAXWELL

THE FALLS OF THE CLYDE

THE GORGE

I DO not know whether the ancients may not have been right in attributing some sort of spirit to a river. If there could be any such thing as a consciousness it is discernible here as the Clyde approaches the great plunge. At Hyndford Bridge, which I have depicted on page 69, this anticipation begins. Perhaps it is a slackening of the waters at the edge of the plateau before the leap is made or it may be pure fancy on the part of the beholder.

Anyhow, if it is not really there, it is there to me.
There is a hush upon the stream and then a distant
noise of waters :

> As he rode ower yon high, high hill,
>   Down by yon dowie den,
> The roar that was in Clyde Water
>   Wad feared five hunerd men.
>
> O roaring Clyde, ye roar ower loud,
>   Your stream seem wonder strang ;
> Make me your prey as I come back,
>   But spare me as I gang.

Bonnington, the first of the falls, is a two-fold, at
times a three-fold, waterfall. The drop is about thirty
feet, but the dramatic setting and the steep tree-
covered walls of the gorge, like cyclopean masonry,
heighten the effect. The falls tumble into the
gorge almost at right angles to its subsequent
course, which is full of rapids and wildly romantic,
until it girds itself for its next great plunge at Corra
Linn.

Of course there is one of the numerous caves in
which Wallace hid. These occur with the same
regularity along the Clyde as beds in which Queen
Elizabeth slept in English manor houses. There is
no need to doubt the authenticity of either. Wallace
is associated with a great many ruins which were not,
as a matter of fact, built in his time, just as Julius
Cæsar is supposed to have made camps which were
really the works of the Saxons many centuries

HYNDFORD BRIDGE

DONALD MAXWELL

after him or of the Celts of many centuries before he came.

I have heard visitors from England refer to the great fall as Corra Linn Falls, but, with all my ignorance of Scotland, I know enough to recognize in this description a redundancy. Linn is, I suppose, the Scottish word for a fall. Further south it means also a deep pool as in Lincoln, King's Lynn, where it cannot mean a fall. In Lynton (Devonshire) the same word appears.

Corra Linn is a wonderfully impressive sight. The water races faster and faster as it gathers impetus for its great leap, and then takes three plunges, each a wilder venture than the one before, and then dives down into a boiling pool which sends up a drifting smoke of water. The sides of the gorge are a mass of waving foliage. Above it, and perched on a crag, is a fragment of ruin seen in dramatic contrast to the hurrying waters. I could wish that the trees that almost hide this feature of the view could be thinned somewhat. It would greatly add to the impressive effect if they were.

Turner alone has given any idea of the vast volume of water pouring down the gorge, and this is in his plate *The Clyde* in the Liber Studiorum. He has done this, however, at some sacrifice to unimportant detail. For instance he has had to introduce something in the way of figures to show the scale, but as to the possibility of actually bathing there I am somewhat sceptical.

I do not know whether Mr. Neil Munro is describing

the Liber Studiorum plate or some other picture of the same subject but he does not seem to have appreciated the great painter's treatment. He writes :

" Turner bathed his fancy in those swirling, rainbow-tinted canopies of spray, and produced a canvas that combines the minimum of natural fact with the maximum of ideal glamour in a fashion that has made it ever since a joy to the adept and a puzzle to the common man."

I feel sorry for the common man. He makes me think of a story told of Turner. An old lady who was introduced to the great Academician ventured to say to him, after much general appreciation, " But do you know, Mr. Turner, I never see in nature what you see."

" Quite so, madam," said Turner, with a twinkle in his eye, " But don't you wish you did ? "

Next time you have an opportunity of going into the Tate Gallery and looking up the Liber Studiorum plate (together with its wonderful etched outline), tell me honestly—although you may modestly class yourself with the " common man " and the Philistine —do you think that any one has been so near rendering the crash and rush and roar of this gorge of Clydesdale ?

Less than a mile below Corra Linn we come to New Lanark and the mills. They are still flourishing but they have had a chequered history before they settled down to their ordered life of to-day. The first mill was built here in 1783 by David Dale and

Arkwright of spinning-jenny fame. Dale's son-in-law was Robert Owen and it was he who tried all sorts of socialistic experiments which, however, as so many of those experiments do, came to nothing. I do not mean to say that they necessarily came to nothing because they were socialistic. It was rather because a great factor had been left out of the movement and

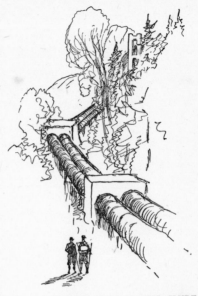

THE NEW FALLS OF THE CLYDE

that was the factor of human nature. Reform would always be so simple if there was no such thing !

Lanark is known to most of the world because of its races. It is of course the best centre for exploring this part of the Clyde, the Mouse Water and the Douglas Water. The New Falls of the Clyde, i.e. the giant pipes down which the water runs to drive turbines instead of pouring over Corra Linn, is situated at a point not far below this fall. It is not in itself unsightly ; in fact it has rather an eerie look like some sort of Wellsian scenery in the moon. The parallel pipes, though on a much bigger scale, remind me of the pipe line from the oil fields in Persia to the Port of Abadan.

The same effect at Stonebyres is not so apparent because from the ordinary approach to the falls they are not visible. The generating station, however, is a building which looks rather pleasant as seen through the trees far below as the traveller descends the precipitous path from the cottage and entrance gate upon the road. It is of a clean white cement and being free from any stains of smoke will not, I think, spoil the scenery. In fact I thought it looked rather a telling object in the sunlight, like an eastern palace hidden in a fairy gorge. Distance lends it mystery if not enchantment.

BONNINGTON FALLS

LOW TIDE AT STONEBYRES

WALLACE LAND

MY impressions of Scotland, of which, as I have said, I know little, are strongest where it differs from the south. To the eyes of a man of Kent, used as they are to russet and red, the colouring of Lanark, as of all these towns, seems a little severe. In the country districts the use of white-wash makes the buildings flash and gleam among the trees and on the hillside, but its comparative rareness in a street tends to monotony.

There is something about Lanark reminiscent of

a Continental town. I do not know quite wherein the likeness lies. It is not in its churches which to me seem to be the last word in gloom and depression. It is not in its people, for every one I spoke to made me feel thoroughly " at home," as everywhere a southern stranger is made to feel (and they knew I was a " foreigner ") when he crosses the border. I think it is something about its situation on top of a hill. Lanark reminded me strongly both of Luxemburg and of Jerusalem. From the east, as the traveller ascends from New Lanark, it looks like Luxemburg. From the road by Stonebyres Linn there is a glimpse of it, set upon a hill, that recalls Jerusalem as seen from the lower valley of the Kedron.

Lector : I wish you would stick to your subject instead of making these highly fanciful comparisons and running down our religion.

Pictor : My dear Lector, I am not running down your religion. I merely said that " to me " the churches of Lanark are the last word in gloom and depression. Perhaps to you they are most exhilarating. I refer of course to the buildings.

Lector : Yes, but you must be careful. Most of your readers will be Scots and the vast majority either Presbyterians or Roman Catholics who regard your church as neither fish nor fowl nor good red herring.

Pictor : I do not mind in the least if they regard my church as a lobster mayonnaise, but I am going to write of my impressions of Scotland and the

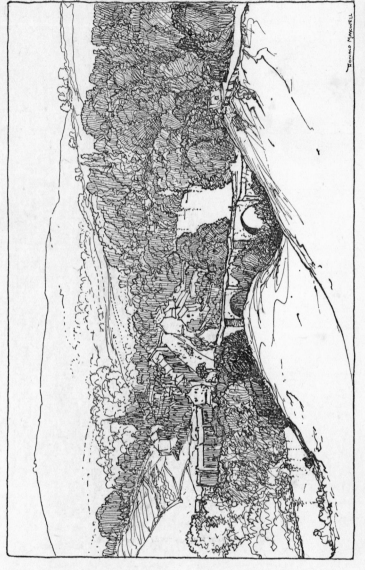

KIRKFIELDBANK

Clyde in my own way. You do not want a colourless
guide book shorn of everything that may offend a
possible buyer. If you are a true descendant of the
Covenanters you will welcome liberty of thought,
and if you are a true Scot you will not give in to a
few hard knocks,[1] but welcome a chance to show
your loyalty to your great poet. Scotsmen love to
see themselves (or their churches) as others see them.

Lector : Pax vobiscum.

Pictor : Et cum spiritu tuo.

Below Lanark as the traveller upon the Clyde's
luxuriant banks descends the hill, a romantic view
of Kirkfieldbank bursts upon his view, most telling
when seen on a grey or hazy day—a jumble of
houses, a spire and a mediæval bridge and far
beyond and above it green hills and banks of trees.
Again below this point and on the right bank the
Mouse Water joins the main river. This emerges
from a chasm of rock with wooded heights, a wonderful byway for the Clyde traveller to explore.

If Miss Jane Porter's romance *Scottish Chiefs* is to
be taken as good history, we are in the very Mecca
of Wallace Land. It was in 1296 :

" Wallace rode on till, crossing the bridge of
Lanark, he saw the rising moon silver the tops of
the distant hills . . . and putting spurs to his horse
. . . he hastened through the town.

" Abruptly turning an angle leading to the Mouse
River, a cry of murder arrested his ear. He checked

---

[1] Several Scottish readers have written to say they object to this allusion
to the Scottish Reformation—and people still say that the Scot has no
sense of humour !

his horse and listened. The clash of arms told him the sound had issued from an alley to the left. . . . On arriving, he discovered two men in tartans, with their backs to the opposite wall, furiously assaulted by a throng of Edward's soldiers."

Then follows a fierce fight in the midst of which a soldier cries out that Arthur Heselrigge is slain and a vow of vengeance upon Wallace is shouted from mouth to mouth. Wallace, although wounded, escapes and gets to his castle, Ellerslie, by means of a way through his garden. The pursuers throng around the walls still shouting for vengeance. Marion, Wallace's wife, urges him to escape. He does this by climbing from one of the windows into a tree and so is lost to sight as the English soldiers burst in.

" ' I am Sir William Wallace's wife,' returned the gentle Marion in a firm tone ; ' and by what authority you seek him thus, and presume to call him guilty, I cannot understand.'

" ' By the authority of the laws, madam, which he has violated.'

" ' What laws ? ' rejoined she. ' Sir William Wallace acknowledges none but those of God and his country. Neither of these has he transgressed."

" The officer replied : ' This night he assassinated Arthur Heselrigge in the streets of Lanark ; and that condemns him, by the last declaration of King Edward : *Whatever Scot maltreats any of the English soldiers, or civil officers, garrisoned in the towns of*

TOM MACLELL

BELOW STONEBYRES

Scotland, shall thereby forfeit his life, as the penalty of his crime.'

" ' A tyrant's law, sir, to which no freeborn Scot will submit ! ' "

Then follows a parley between the brave Marion and Sir Gilbert Hambledon. He treats her with chivalry and although leaving a guard to watch in case of Wallace's return, withdraws from the scene. Wallace finds refuge in a cave by Corra Linn.

In the morning, however, the uncle of the dead Heselrigge appears.

"Woman ! " cried he, " I am the governor of Lanark. You now stand before the representative of the great King Edward ; and on your allegiance to him, and on peril of your life, I command you to answer me three questions. Where is Sir William Wallace, and the murderer of my nephew ? Who is that old Scot for whom my nephew was slain ? He and his whole family shall meet my vengeance ! And tell me where is that box of treasure which your husband stole from Douglas Castle ? Answer me these questions on your life."

In blind rage because Lady Marion refuses to reply, Heselrigge plunges his sword into her heart. An aged retainer carries the news of this foul murder to Wallace in the cave by Corra Linn.

" Huge masses of rock, canopied with a thick umbrage of firs, beech and weeping birch, closed over the glen and almost excluded the light of day. But more anxious as he calculated by the increased rapidity of the stream he must now be approaching the great fall near his master's concealment, Halbert redoubled his speed. . . .

" Fearful of being overwhelmed by the streams, which now on all sides crossed his path, he kept upon the edge of the river, to be as far as possible from their violence. And thus he proceeded, slowly and with trepidation, through numerous defiles and under the plunge of many a mountain-torrent till the augmented storm of a world of waters, dashing from side to side, and boiling up with the noise and fury of the contending elements above, told him he was indeed not far from the fall of Corie Lynn."

When Wallace learns the dreadful fate of his wife he dedicates his life to the cause of vengeance and the liberation of Scotland. Rallying his followers he attacks the castle of Lanark and slays the murderer in his quarters at the northern gate.

STONEBYRES LINN

MILK AND HONEY

BELOW Stonebyres Linn, the river takes a course more or less north-west, and then, by Crossford, enters a broader region of the valley. A more placid form of landscape commences, and the Clyde, now flowing amidst fields and crops, takes to looping backwards and forwards. A domestic touch is given to the scenery and many acres of strawberry plantations and market gardens for the supplying of Glasgow begin to be the dominating note upon its banks.

This is a land of orchards and fruit, of dazzling blossom in the spring and of loaded branches in the autumn. Apples, pears, plums abound upon the slopes of the Clyde, and strawberries, gooseberries and raspberries and all manner of succulent vegetable crops upon the flat green lands that fringe the river. I am told that strawberry growing is an industry of comparatively recent date and that fifty years ago it was almost unknown and regarded as a " new-fangled " and risky business. The acreage now under strawberries alone is considerable and the picking season employs people from the villages and from Glasgow in the same manner as the annual hopping holiday for the Londoner in Kent.

The strawberry crop is heaviest from the lowest levels of the valley and increases inversely as the height of the land from the river level, after the manner of the law of gravitation. Hundreds of acres of tomatoes are grown under glass between here and Glasgow. Did we not know that this is an entirely new industry we might have been for-given as wild guessers of place-names to attribute the very name of the great city to this profusion of greenhouses upon the slopes of the Clyde.

Into this peaceful zone of the valley come streams from wilder gorges. The Nethan Water is the most notable of these, and it is familiar to all because of *Old Mortality* and the Tower of Tillietudlem.

The walls of Craignethan appear romantically among the trees of the steep banks of the stream, and we remember that it was here that Sir Walter

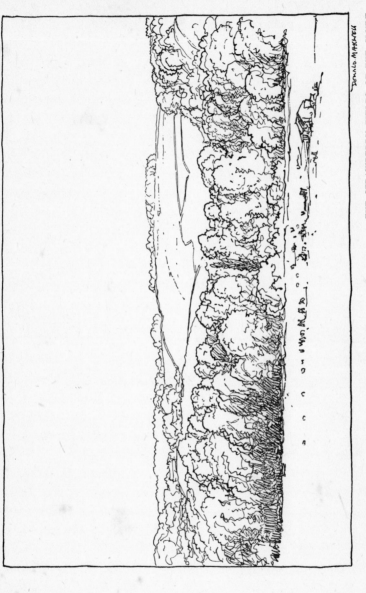

Donald MAXWELL

THE STRAWBERRY FIELDS OF THE CLYDE

Scott nearly decided to make his home instead of at
Abbotsford. The water in the bed of the Nethan
is of a browner colour than that of the Clyde, a
phenomenon which is caused by the peat bogs in the
bare and lonely country above it.

Here is the description of Craignethan Castle as
the Tower of Tillietudlem [1] :

" The Tower of Tillietudlem stood, or perhaps yet
stands, upon the angle of a very precipitous bank,
formed by the junction of a considerable brook with
the Clyde. The fortalice . . . had been in times of
war a post of considerable importance, the possession
of which was necessary to secure communication of
the upper and wilder districts of the country with
those beneath, where the valley expands and is more
capable of cultivation. The view downwards is of
a grand wooded character, but the level ground and
gentle slopes near the river form cultivated fields of
an irregular shape, interspersed with hedge-row
trees and copses, the enclosures seeming to have
been individually cleared out of the forest which
surrounds them and which occupies, in unbroken
masses, the steeper declivities and more distant
banks. The stream, in colour a clear and sparkling
brown like the hue of Cairngorm pebbles, rushes
through this romantic region in bold sweeps and
curves, partly visible and partly concealed by the
trees which clothe its banks. With a providence

[1] It will be remembered that the railway company is responsible for the
name of this station here, not the map. Scott's name is fictitious. There
is a Gillytudlem below Lanark and this was no doubt the model for the
coined name, Tillietudlem.

93

unknown in other parts of Scotland, the peasants have, in most places, planted orchards around their cottages ; and the general blossom of the apple-trees . . . gives all the lower part of the view the appearance of a flower-garden. Looking up the river, the character of the scene varies considerably for the worse. A hilly waste and uncultivated country approached close to the banks ; the trees were few and limited to the neighbourhood of the stream ; and the rude moors swelled at a little distance into shapeless and heavy hills, which were again surmounted in their turn by a range of lofty mountains, dimly seen on the horizon. Thus the tower commanded two prospects—the one richly cultivated and highly adorned, the other exhibiting the monotonous and dreary character of a wild and inhospitable moorland."

Not far below this part of the river and only a few miles to the west, the Avon flows in a winding course more or less parallel to the Clyde and joins it at Hamilton. The ruins of the ancient residence of the Hamiltons are to be found on the steep banks of this tributary river about two miles above its mouth.

The solemn sylvan scenery that enshrines these ancient walls, darkened as they are by foliage and creeping plants and by trees that overhang the river, is romantic and impressive. Beyond the fact that this ancient castle was a royal residence in the time of Alexander II, little about its early history is to be found.

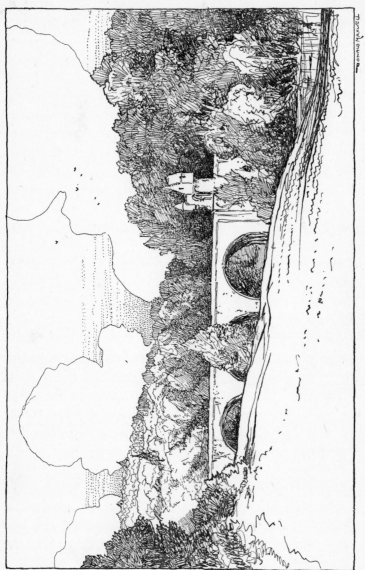

MILTON LOCKHART

In Sir Walter Scott's stirring ballad *Cadzow Castle*,
Bothwellhaugh suddenly appears on horseback
among his kinsmen who were hunting in Cadzow
Forest, after the assassination of the Regent Murray
at Linlithgow. The following verses depict the
scene :

> When princely Hamilton's abode
>   Ennobled Cadzow's Gothic towers,
> The song went round, the goblet flowed,
>   And revel sped the laughing hours.
>
> Then, thrilling to the harp's gay sound,
>   So sweetly sung each vaulted wall,
> And echoed light the dancer's bound
>   As mirth and music cheered the hall,
>
> .   .   .   .   .
>
> But see, the minstrel's vision fails,
>   The glimmering spears are seen no more :
> The shouts of war die on the gales
>   Or sink in Avon's lovely roar.
>
> For loud the bugle, pealing high
>   The black bird whistles down the vale ;
> And sunk in vivid ruins lie,
>   The bannered towers of Avondale.

The oaks of Cadzow were said to have been planted
by David, Earl of Huntingdon (afterwards King of
Scotland) in 1140.   I have turned up the following
interesting reference in an old (and undated) book
entitled *Our Own Country* :

" It is from an incident in the life of Walter de

Hamilton, the first of his race who possessed Cadzow, that the Hamiltons (so it is asserted) derive their crest which still surmounts their shield—a tree half-sawn, with the motto ' Through.' This Hamilton, being at the Court of Edward II, managed to contract a feud with the Dispensers, and was obliged to take flight. He was closely pursued, and at one time he and his servant found it necessary to change clothes with some workmen, who were cutting down a tree, and to take their places. The pursuers went by ; and, as the servant looked after them uneasily, Sir Walter, to divert his attention, called out ' Through,' and the tree soon fell."

Sir Walter Scott makes the age of these oaks still greater, unless this is merely poetic license. In his allusion to the famous white cattle of Cadzow he writes :

> Through the huge oaks of Evandale,
>   Whose limbs a thousand years have worn,
> What sullen roar comes down the gale
>   And drowns the hunter's pealing horn ?
>
> Mightiest of all the beasts of chase,
>   That roam in woody Caledon,
> Crashing the forest in his race
>   The mountain bull comes thundering on.

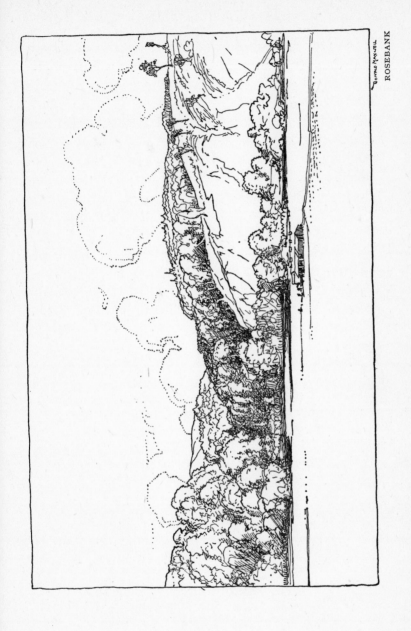

ROSEBANK

'BOTHWELL BANK THOU BLUMEST FAYRE'

BELOW the region of orchards and market gardens beginning at Crossford the valley suddenly narrows at Milton Lockhart, where the romantic bridge with its fairy-tale gate-house spans the stream (page 95) and where Maudesley Castle lies hidden in its ramparts of trees. Then the strip of flat land spreads out again at Rosebank and the hills retire, yet falling richly and tree-covered to the waters' edge.

Scots people will know of the romance hidden in

the name of Lockhart, but it is probable that many of my readers from the south will not. The effigy of the Lockhart family is the Heart within a Fetterlock. This tells of the time when their famous ancestor, Sir Simon of Lee, became the guardian of the heart of Bruce, when his leader fell in a fight with the Moors as he and his party were on the way to Palestine.

> Lord James of Douglas, mark my side,
>   That heart shall pass once more
> In fiery fight against the foe
>   As it was wont of yore.
>
> And it shall pass beneath the Cross
>   And save King Robert's vow,
> But other hands shall bear it back,
>   Not, James of Douglas, thou !
>
> Now by thy mighty faith, I pray,
>   Sir Simon of the Lee—
> For truer friend hath never man
>   Than thou hast been to me—
>
> If ne'er upon the Holy Land
>   'Tis mine in life to tread,
> Bear thou to Scotland's kindly earth
>   The relics of her dead.[1]

There is a delightful water-mill a mile or so below Milton Lockhart. I have sketched this on page 103, and on the river Avon above this point where it joins the Clyde is a glimpse of bridges which I have

---

[1] *Lays of the Scottish Cavaliers* (W. E. Aytoun).

A WATER-MILL ABOVE HAMILTON

drawn on page 107. Hamilton, renowned in history and sought after by travellers because of its Palace, is now a region of smoke and slag heaps—with little bursts of charming scenery in between.

The Clyde now flows through places the names of which are familiar not only to Scotland but to the whole world. Bothwell Castle and Bothwell Bridge are known wherever the Clyde is known. Every memory of our history books, to say nothing of the pages of *Old Mortality* make us strangely at home as we wander up and down the tree-covered banks with the great castle on one side and the gaunt ruins of Blantyre Priory on the other.

In spite of the encroachment of the coal industry and the nearness of all this riverside seclusion to the roar and clang of Hamilton and Motherwell, there is still to be found peace and quiet under the walls of Blantyre and the red bastions of Bothwell.

The crumbling towers of this venerable ruin are to the west of the present mansion. They stand challengingly upon the steep green bank of the river. " The oldest part of this rambling pile, although very little of it is left how, became known to history in the early part of the thirteenth century, and was a great baronial stronghold in the stirring times of Wallace and Bruce."

A circular vault under the inner side of the front wall, about twenty feet deep and twelve feet in diameter, appears to have been used as a prison and bears popularly the name of " Wallace's Beef Barrel." Traces of the fosse which encompassed the castle are still visible. The adjacent ground on the east side is now laid out in garden form and is ablaze with flowers.

> The tufted grass lines Bothwell's ancient hall,
> The fox peeps cautious from the crowded wall ;
> Where once proud Murray, Clydesdale's ancient lord,
> A mimic sovereign, held the festal board.

There is little left about the scant walls of Blantyre to suggest a monastery. The original buildings were those of a cell of the Abbey of Jedburgh, and tradition says that this was a secret retreat useful when the border raids of the English became too hot to be tolerated.

Its suppression at the Reformation brought it into the possession of Walter Stewart, afterwards Lord Blantyre. Such fragments of the ruins as are to be seen to-day are for the most part relics of the mansion that he used as an occasional summer residence.

Whenever there are two ancient buildings anywhere near each other it is inevitable that there will be a story of a secret passage linking the two together. Miss Jane Porter's romance, *The Scottish Chiefs*, makes use of this supposed connexion. It has often been referred to by other writers. These secret passages almost invariably belong to the past. They never exist as relics to be seen to-day. I have myself the gravest doubts as to their existence at any time where the distance is great or the engineering problem difficult, as in this case, tunnelling beneath a river.

BRIDGES ON THE AVON

It is not an infrequent thing that some sort of a tunnel is found underneath monastic buildings. It is naturally supposed to be the remains of some secret passage. As a matter of fact the explanation is a prosaic one. According to an architect friend of mine they are generally the remains of drains. Often a water channel has been run underneath a building and this conduit has been used as a drainage system.

The comparative immunity enjoyed by the monasteries in many of the plague visitations that swept over Europe is to be attributed largely to the fact that they had some sort of sanitation whereas the outside world had none.

Bothwell Bridge is now modernized. I have sketched one aspect of it as seen from the right bank about a mile above it (page 111). In the days of the battle of Bothwell Bridge, however, there was a gate with portcullis in the centre and this was the key to the battle. Had the Covenanters been able to keep the bridge the day might have been different. It is doubtful, nevertheless, whether the ranks of the Presbyterian army could have held together for long in any case, owing to the mad fanaticism that divided their councils. The more moderate leaders, those who really did want religious freedom and not merely the power to impose their tyranny on others, were overborne by the majority. A monument to this minority of wise and brave men—at least so I interpret the inscription—stands to-day at the northern approach to the bridge. Here is a quotation from *Old Mortality* which gives a vivid account of the defence of the bridge :

" Monmouth, mounted on a superb white charger, might be discovered on the top of the right bank of the river, urging, entreating, and animating the exertion of his soldiers. By his orders, the cannon which had hitherto been employed in annoying the distant main body of the Presbyterians were now turned upon the defenders of the bridge. But these tremendous engines, being wrought much more slowly than in modern times, did not produce the effect of annoying or terrifying the enemy to the extent proposed. The insurgents, sheltered by copsewood along the bank of the river, or stationed in the houses already mentioned, fought under cover, while the royalists, owing to the precautions of Morton, were entirely exposed. The defence was so protracted and obstinate, that the royal generals began to fear it might be ultimately successful. While Monmouth threw himself from his horse, and, rallying the Foot Guards, brought them to another close and desperate attack, he was warmly seconded by Dalzell, who, putting himself at the head of a body of Lennox-Highlanders, rushed forward with their tremendous war-cry of Loch-sloy. The ammunition of the defenders of the bridge began to fail at this important crisis ; messages commanding and imploring succours and supplies were in vain despatched, one after the other, to the main body of the Presbyterian army, which remained inactively drawn up on the open fields in the rear. Fear,

DONALD MAXWELL

BOTHWELL BRIDGE

consternation, and misrule had gone abroad among them, and while the post on which their safety depended required to be instantly and powerfully reinforced, there remained none either to command or to obey.

" As the first of the defenders of the bridge began to slacken, that of the assailants increased, and in its turn became more fatal. Animated by the example and exhortations of their generals, they obtained a footing upon the bridge itself, and began to remove the obstacles by which it was blockaded. The portal-gate was broken open, the beams, trunks of trees, and other materials of the barricade pulled down and thrown into the river. This was not accomplished without opposition. . . . The passage being now open, the enemy began to pour over. But the bridge was long and narrow, which rendered the manœuvre slow as well as dangerous ; and those who first passed had still to force the houses, from the windows of which the Covenanters continued to fire. . . .

" In the meanwhile, the forces of the king crossed the bridge at their leisure, and, securing the pass, formed in line of battle ; while Claverhouse, who, like a hawk perched on a rock, and eyeing the time to pounce on its prey, had watched the event of the action from the opposite bank, now passed the bridge at the head of his cavalry, at full trot, and, leading them in squadrons through the intervals and round the flanks of the royal infantry, formed them in line on the moor, and led them to the charge, advancing in front with one large body, while other two divisions threatened the flanks of the Covenanters. . . . The front ranks hardly attempted one ill-directed and disorderly fire, and their rear were broken and flying in confusion ere the charge had been completed ; and in less than five minutes the horsemen were mixed with them, cutting and hewing without mercy. The voice of Claverhouse was heard, even above the din of conflict, exclaiming to his soldiers : ' Kill, kill—no quarter—think on Richard Grahame ! ' The dragoons, many of whom had shared the disgrace of Louden Hill, required no exhortations to vengeance as easy as it was complete. Their swords drank deep of slaughter among the unresisting fugitives. Screams for quarter were only answered by the shouts with which the pursuers accompanied their blows, and the whole field presented one general scene of confused slaughter, flight, and pursuit."

It had always seemed strange to me that Monmouth, whose part in crushing the enemies of " popery " must have been well known, should have been accepted within a few years in the West of England as the champion of Protestantism. His easy success at Bothwell Bridge may have given him false confidence as a leader and led him on to be beaten ignominiously at Sedgemoor and finally beheaded.

BOTHWELL CASTLE
FROM BLANTYRE PRIORY

THE CITY OF SHIPS

BELOW Hamilton and Bothwell, the Clyde enters a region that has very little individuality. Once a beautiful riverside and still showing from time to time their old-time characteristics, the banks of the river are now in many places indistinguishable from the banks of any other river of a great manufacturing and industrial centre. Parts of it might be in Wigan, parts in London, parts in Middlesbrough, parts in Liverpool—and few parts there be that suggest Scotland to the traveller.

There is Cambuslang where a small stream known as the Kirk-burn joins the Clyde. The old name of the place is Thief's Ford. In the New Statistical account there is reference to a great religious movement in 1742 in which Whitfield figured prominently. The Revival (as it would be called to-day) is known as " The Cambuslang Wark." Here is a reference :

" The sacrament was given twice in the space of five weeks, on the 11th of July and on the 15th of August. Mr. Whitfield had arrived from England in June, and many of the most popular preachers of the day hastened to join him at Cambuslang. . . . The sacrament on the 15th August was very numerously attended. One tent was placed at the lower extremity of the amphitheatre above alluded to, near the joining of the two rivulets, and here the sacrament was administered. A second tent was erected in the churchyard and a third in a green field a little to the west of the first tent. Each of these was attended with great congregations and it has been estimated that not less than 30,000 people attended on that occasion. Four ministers preached on the Fast-day, four on Saturday, fourteen or fifteen on Sunday, five on Monday. There were 25 tables, about 120 at each, in all, 3,000 communicants."

In contrast to this religious activity is a sad story of backsliding at Rutherglen. I cannot give you the exact date of the occurrence, but it happened, so the story goes, during the ministry of Mr. Dickson " who suffered sair during the persecution." He was riding up the main street at midnight. " While passing along the kirk-yard wall, he fancied, to his surprise, that he heard sounds of merriment issuing from his own church. Being a man of some courage,

BOTHWELL CASTLE
ACROSS THE CLYDE

he at once dismounted from his steed, made his way into the grave-yard, which was then, as now, elevated, with its time-honoured elms, a few feet above the level of the street, and looking into the sacred edifice, which was lighted up as if for a festival, beheld to his horror and amazement, several of his own congregation, male and female, engaged

A TOWER OF BOTHWELL

in some mysterious ceremony, in company with a gentleman in black, whom he at once knew, from a well-known peculiarity of foot, as the enemy of mankind. Provoked beyond forbearance at the desecration of his church, and the evident backsliding of a portion of his flock, he roared out with the voice of a stentor, " Ye'll no deny this the morn, ye Limmers ! " '

He then rode away, but was overtaken by the powers of darkness, who turned both horse and rider into stone. " Stock-still they were compelled to stand, unable to move hand or foot, nor would the band of warlocks and witches release them from this statuesque state, but on condition that his reverence would give his solemn pledge never to divulge the names of those whom he had discovered in such questionable company. This, although with reluctance, he was ultimately fain to do." [1]

My sympathies, of course, are entirely on the side of Mr. Dickson, but had the promise not been given Glasgow might have been the richer by even yet another equestrian statue and possibly it would have been an improvement on many of those that it already possesses.

The Clyde in Glasgow itself, above the bridges, is a river sadly marred. It flows cheerlessly past the Green, that open space which is to Glasgow what Hyde Park and Trafalgar Square are to London, Nelson Monument included. Here James Watt, according to common report, thought out his invention of the steam engine—and on the Sabbath.

It does not come within the province of this short book to give any impressions of Glasgow, save only as it affects the town scenery of the river banks. Some of this is disappointing, but the unexpected views in this region of the docks are numerous.

[1] *Rambles Round Glasgow* (Hugh Macdonald).

THE GOLDEN WAY

"STANDS SCOTLAND WHERE SHE DID ?"

Giant mills suddenly appear above mean houses and a dash of colour or a dazzle of white often break the monotony of an otherwise grey street scene. By night especially can be seen strange effects. I have endeavoured to show one of these in a nocturne of old Glasgow (page 127) where the University and the venerable buildings of the city make a towering skyline above the river.

One Saturday evening, when everything was very still and when the usual hum and bustle of the sheds and wharves had died down, I came upon a scene (page 123) that shows the Glasgow Clyde at sunset. There was no one about but the inevitable policeman and occasional passer-by from one of the vessels lying there. The sun was low and there appeared a grand canal of glittering water, between cliffs of great steamers upon either shore. The distance was lost in sunny haze and it seemed as if a great highway opened out across the world. China, Newfoundland, Borneo, India, the green ranches of South America, the golden grain-lands of Canada—all these lay just down there and the gaunt forests of these shipyards were nothing more than magic contrivances by which the ant-like industry of man could link these countries to our shores.

On another evening I came upon a wonderful picture, an even more striking effect. Twilight was falling and rain filled the sky and glittered in the roadways. I was driving from Renfrew into Glasgow, when I saw in the heavens, faint and immensely high and striding as it were across the city, spider-like monsters, H. G. Wells's fantastic creatures from Mars. They were the faintly descried traceries of a shipyard and its giant cranes. And yet there are people who will tell an artist that he will find no subjects of romance till he gets clear of Glasgow streets.

A NOCTURNE OF GLASGOW

THE ROAD TO EVERYWHERE

THE name Broomielaw holds the same pleasant reminder for Glasgow that Saffron Hill has for London. In either case a few gaudy posters are the only means of bringing to the landscape either the colour of broom in flower or of saffron. Yet Broomielaw, unlike Saffron Hill, is the gate to delectable mountains and the " open sesame " to enchanted waters. For it is here that the citizen of Glasgow can at any time, by passing through a turnstile, become a Christopher Columbus all by himself and discover new worlds of beauty, or he can, as the psalmist of old, lift up his eyes to the hills whence cometh his help.

Glasgow without a steamboat service would seem to shrink considerably. The loyal Glasgow dweller, when faced with the superior architectural merits of Edinburgh, can always retaliate, " Yes, but we have the Kyles of Bute." The Kyles of Bute are Glasgow's greatest boast, speaking " touristically," and the name itself is almost as valuable as the scenery, because it is one of the few place-names in Scotland pronounced in the same way by the English visitor and by his Scottish host.

I know a man who journeyed half over Scotland trying to find a delightful spot called Kirran. A native of the place, whom he had met on his travels, described its charms so vividly that he decided to go there at all costs. " Now, remember," his mentor reiterated as they parted, " Kirran. In case you dinna mind it write it doon." My friend wrote it down at once KIRRAN in his note-book. He was rather mystified as to why he should write it down whether he minded it or not. If what this enthusiastic native described were in any way true, he would not mind it at all. He would quite *like* it. The Scotch he thought were strange people. Did they think because he came from London and was unused to mountains and lakes that he would *mind* them ? He would like them all the more because they were to him so different from the humdrum suburban environment of his own home.

He never found Kirran, however, but he came one

ERSKINE FERRY

day to a place named Kirn ; there it was—KIRN, on a board as large as life. It was extraordinarily like the place he was looking for. In fact, every point in the landscape fitted perfectly. So he stayed there instead and had a delightful holiday. If ever he meets his would-be guide again, he will tell him that Kirran is not the only place with the unique charms so patriotically advocated. Kirn could boast everything of these scenic joys and more also.

If the advocate of the superior architectural charms of Edinburgh is not sufficiently crushed by the Kyles of Bute he is side-tracked and left without power of retaliation by the statement that Glasgow is the second city in the Kingdom. This argument, however, although often effective is not original. Other people in different parts of the world have tried that dodge. I remember once when I was in Bombay complaining of the trying dampness of the heat and an enthusiastic resident of old standing replied that Bombay was the second city in the Empire. The statement did not seem to make it any cooler, but I was too exhausted to argue and I let it pass. In fact I made a mental note of the fact for future reference. A few months after this I chanced to be in Calcutta and complained to an old resident and motorist that the taxi-drivers seemed to me to be the most reckless and terrible fellows I had ever seen, and wondered what was the average life of a motorist who crossed the Maidan every day. He replied with dignity that Calcutta was the second city in the Empire.

After these two experiences it is not to be wondered at that I am not impressed by the argument of size alone.

In the middle ages Glasgow was a small town upon the north bank of the Clyde, built irregularly upon the rising ground on which stands the Cathedral. The south side of the river consisted of pastures and a few scattered farms. As the city grew the importance of Greenock and Port Glasgow grew also, for there were the landing places of goods which were unloaded at these wharves and sent by road to the city, and also floated in shallow-draught lighters up the river. No one, however, seems to have seen the necessity of taking ships right up into Glasgow or the engineering difficulties were considered to be insuperable. An attempt at getting a near port for the unloading of seagoing vessels was made by a request to the authorities of Dumbarton to become a clearing house to the city. But Dumbarton was very doubtful. The offer was declined. The objection put forward was that the great number of extra inhabitants, to wit, the crews of the ships unloading there, would send up the cost of provisions.

This refusal turned the attention of the people of Glasgow to the possibilities of a deeper and more navigable Clyde. In 1566 a scheme for the dredging of the sandbank at Dumbuck was devised and six years later a newly-erected Harbour Authority began building a quay at the Broomielaw. This was really a very small affair, but it was regarded in those

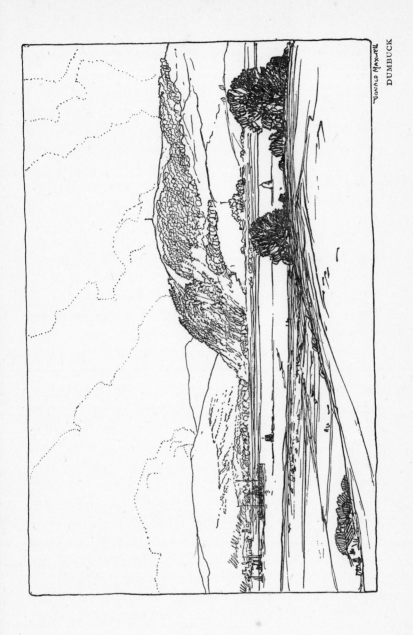

DUMBUCK

DONALD MAXWELL

times as a wonder of progress and modernity. It was made on the north side of the river at a place near the Jamaica Bridge of to-day. We find from records that wood from the cathedral was voted to keep it in repair, which act shows one of two things, that the people of Glasgow in 1663 thought a great deal of their quay or very little of their cathedral. Things went on very much in this small way until 1840, when the importance of making Glasgow more accessible to the sea was keenly felt. The Clyde Navigation Trust was formed. The improvements made were steady and continuous. In 1854 began the removal of the rock ledge at Elderslie, a long affair, on and off, which was only finally completed at the beginning of this century. Compared with the conditions of to-day when ships of some thirty feet draught can make Glasgow, the navigation of the river was still in its infancy, although it is amusing and instructive to note how each improvement was hailed as the very last word in progress and there is a note almost of finality in some of the pæans of praise which were accorded to Scotland's engineers. The most amusing of all is Hugh Macdonald's mild and humorous rebuke (1854) to the over enthusiasm of " old M'Ure" who wrote in (about) 1720 :

> More pure than amber is the river Clyde
> Whose gentle streams do by thy borders glide ;
> And here a thousand sail receive commands
> To traffic for thee into foreign lands.

He writes : " Considering the depth of the river at this period, we have our suspicions that the good old man must have exercised this poetic license to its full extent in his enumeration of the shipping, and that he must have had Dumbarton and Greenock in his eye when he talked of ' foreign lands '. This is all the more likely as we find that a few years earlier, Patrick Bryce, tacksman of the Gorbals coal-heugh, complained that he could not get his coals loaded at the Broomielaw, from the scarcity of water, and that he had to crave license from Sir George Maxwell to have them transported through the lands of Pollok to a place of embarkation near Meikle Goran." He goes on to picture the astonish-ment of both " the enterprising coalmaster " and " the sage historian " if they could now see the wonders of Clyde navigation to day (1854).

" And now such ' leviathans afloat ' as the *Glasgow* (1,152 tons) and the *Simla* steam unimpeded down its course."

It would be interesting in turn for us to imagine the astonishment and wonder of Hugh Macdonald after another 63 years of progress.

If Clyde navigation goes on growing at the rate it has done in the last hundred years, no doubt our descendants in like manner will conjure up visions of the old captains of the Clyde in our days. They will imagine them come to life again and gazing in spellbound astonishment at the Clyde shipping of 2027—those old fellows, who thought they were so modern and progressive with their pigmy little

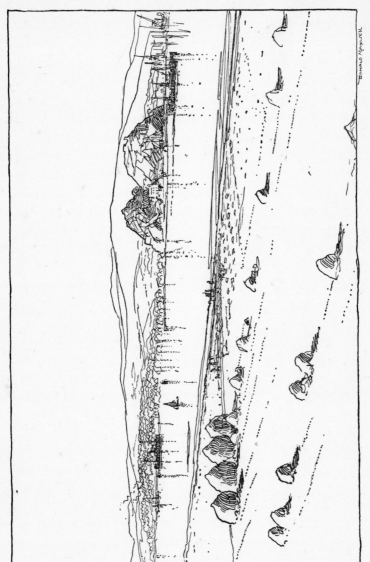

DUMBARTON, FROM LANGBANK

steamships plodding along laboriously amidst primitive smoke and grime. What would they think now of our twenty-million-ton radio liners arriving in fleets from New Zealand where ten minutes previously they had weighed anchor ?

The banks of the Clyde below dockland begin to open out. The hills come into sight, ethereal and blue. The spires of Renfrew on one side and the wooded heights upon the other make backgrounds to the busy scenes in shipyard after shipyard. There are a dozen views which might have in the foreground a scene as at page 129 and the noise of the riveters has no sooner grown faint in one place, when it arises in deafening crescendo in another.

At Erskine Ferry there is a magnificent anticipation of good things to come. My sketch on page 139 was made from the left bank of the river and at the approach to the ferry landing. Upon the hill on the right, across the river, I could discern something in the way of earthworks that looks like a camp or walled enclosure. I think it shows sufficiently in the drawing for the reader to see where he can follow it up if he wishes. It is not far below this point that the Forth and Clyde canal joins the river and the name of Old Kilpatrick will be noted by every true Irishman, for near this spot was born his Patron Saint. It is here, too, on the summit of Castle Hill, that there is a Roman fort and part of the great wall known as " Graham's Dyke "—of which we have just noticed traces, which marches from here across to the Forth for a distance of twenty-six miles.

This immense bulwark against the troublesome peoples of the north was begun by Agricola and finished by Antonine. A great deal of this great work has been obliterated and disguised by the work of building and of agriculture, but the traces which still exist have enabled archæologists to reconstruct it for us. It had no less than nineteen forts upon it which were linked together by a road.

The road from this point at the ferry runs pleasantly along towards Langbank and soon the traveller can see a broad view of the river with its high woods upon the other side (page 135) and the first sight of Dumbarton Rock is discovered, that Gibraltar of the Clyde and landmark of Scottish history.

THE GIBRALTAR OF SCOTLAND

PORT GLASGOW

THE FAIRY SHIPYARDS

THE comparison often made between Dumbarton and Gibraltar is made merely because
a steep precipice stands up from the water and
emphasizes a certain physical resemblance between
the two places. But there is another likeness, a
likeness in story. Not only has this basalt rock held
a garrison since the Act of Union, but at the end of
the fifteenth century it was the chief naval base for
Scotland. To-day in some aspects of light and shade
I have noticed a vivid family likeness caused by the
proximity of shipbuilding activities in one case and
the Dockyard in the other, both at the foot of
precipitous heights.

145

The river Leven runs into the Clyde by this rock, but the somewhat dingy waters that flow through the roaring activities of Dumbarton's works do not suggest that they have come from the bonnie, bonnie banks of Loch Lomond.

Below Langbank, where the road runs along the river and gives delightful views of the hill country across the water, there appears a curious feature. This is a foreshore of innumerable small stakes, in rows and squares and companies. They are as numerous as reeds upon the shores of an inland lake and continue for miles towards Port Glasgow. At first I took them for net stakes, but a closer inspection proved this guess to be wrong. They are evidently enclosures for keeping floating timber. Many acres of these palisaded lakes are obsolete, and the derelict, broken and thinned stake-hedges look more than ever like giant rushes upon some strange shore.

At one place was a hut built on piles and this made me think of the Lake Villages of prehistoric man— although I have not the least idea what these latter villages were like.

By moonlight this shore looks still stranger, and it would be easy to see in it some fantastic suggestion that the fairies, not to be outdone by modern Clyde-side shipbuilding, here started fairy slipways where they build fairy ships for voyages to nowhere.

Lector. You have left out Elderslie where William Wallace was born.

Pictor. Yes, I know, but I can't make this a mere guide book.

"RONALD MAKOUL"

'THE LAKE DWELLINGS' OF THE CLYDE

FAIRY SHIPYARD

Lector. But, you have put in about St. Patrick?

Pictor. All right then, but I refuse to quote Burns. I haven't room and I can only understand him here and there.

William Wallace was born at Elderslie which we have passed. There is little now for the pilgrim to see. There is Wallace's Yew still green, and a stone with initials W.W.W. which was dug up from the foundations of the garden wall is now to be seen at Houston House. Wallace's Oak was blown down in 1856. The trunk was removed by Mr. Speirs of Elderslie and kept as a relic. It cannot now be traced. This is the oak corresponding to the one in which Charles II of England hid when he was pursued. In this case Wallace was in danger from the English. There is, as I have said, very little of Wallace's Elderslie to see and therefore with Campbell I complain that the river no more through pastoral scenes should glide, "My Wallace's own stream and once romantic Clyde." But let us return to Port Glasgow. This place as its name discloses is a created port. In 1688, after the shortsighted decision of

PORT GLASGOW

Dumbarton not to adapt itself to become a port for Glasgow, the merchants of that city purchased thirteen acres of land and built a town and harbour. The venture was instantly a success ; a graving dock, the first in Scotland, was an attraction and ships flocked thither, especially from America and the West Indies. The advent and growth of steam expanded it still more and the little town was altered and added to till it became what it is to-day, a grim place, crowded and unlovely, but with a glorious view of most enchanting scenery. Newark was practically swept away and the old castle, the ancestral fortress of the Maxwells of Danyelstoun, was left stranded and somewhat forlorn. It still looks down upon the encroaching tide of activity around it, perhaps somewhat scornfully after its five hundred years of overlordship.

I have never seen so many children anywhere as in the streets of Port Glasgow. Until half-past ten there were still swarms of small boys and girls playing about on the pavements and doorsteps. I don't know what time people go to bed here. I did not stay up to see. A great number of ships are on the slips and I should imagine work is pretty plentiful. A large Irish population exists here, as in most " shippy " towns on this side of Britain.

It is delightful in warm and sunny weather to turn away from the streets of Port Glasgow and sit upon the quay by the lighthouse. Ships glide by so near that a good biscuit-thrower could almost literally deposit a biscuit upon the deck of a passing

TOWARDS LOCH LOMOND

steamer. The outward-bound vessels seem to leave Dumbarton Rock and make straight for Port Glasgow. There are two lighthouses, painted red. One of these is on the quay, a tall slender one. The other is in the water, a short fat one. These two in line are evidently a bearing. After an alarmingly rapid approach, and when the unnautical stranger thinks a grounding is imminent, the ships bear away a little to starboard and pursue their way towards the point at Gourock.

I know of no spot so delightful to a painter of ships. This quay would make a veritable studio. And away and beyond this procession of the trade of many nations there is a distance of an entrancing beauty ; the blue mountains and the green shores where lie Helensburgh and Roseneath and the heights that overhang Loch Long.

In the early part of the eighteenth century Greenock was no more than a fishing village. Now it is one of the most important of Scotland's towns. It refines sugar and builds ships. Its docks are considerable too, but since Glasgow has done so much to get ships docked at home these have declined somewhat.

Wordsworth compared Greenock to Tyre, and seems to have found in it the Utopia of Scotland.

We have not passed into a doleful City,
We who were led to-day down a grim dell,
By some too boldly called the " Jaws of Hell ! "
Where be the wretched ones, the sights for pity ?

These crowded streets resound no plaintive ditty ;
As from the hive where bees in summer dwell,
Sorrow seems here excluded ; and that knell,
It neither damps the gay nor checks the witty.

To-day, however, Greenock seems to me to be
more in the mood of John Davidson when he wrote :

. . . Here daily dawn
Burns through the smoky east ; with fire-shod feet
The sun treads heaven, and steps from hill to hill
Downward before the night that still pursues
His crimson wake.

GREENOCK

GOUROCK

THE THRESHOLD OF THE HILLS

THE overthrow of the Stewarts in 1688 and
the accession of Dutch William was received
in Scotland with mixed feelings. At Gourock,
however, any disappointment that might have been
felt in certain sections of the community was more
than counterbalanced by the discovery in that
year of the art of smoking herrings. This discovery
was the beginning of great prosperity to the fishing
industry, and Scotch herrings caused the name of
Scotland to be respected by those who knew little
of her prowess of arms.

From time immemorial, even before the discovery

of smoked herrings (an epoch-making invention, the originality of which, I believe, is fiercely contested by Great Yarmouth) the port of Gourock was always considered a lucky one from which to set sail. This luck was attributed to a stone (alleged to be Druidical) about six feet high, and known as " Granny Kempoch." It stands at Kempoch Point, where Gourock joins Ashton.

Granny Kempoch is still beloved of sailors, and many a steamship sounds her syren as she passes, in gratitude for a safe return if she is homeward bound and to keep good luck on the voyage if she is bound outward.

In the old days of sailing ships it was a firm tradition that ballast from Gourock shore would enable any ship to weather the stormiest sea. The veneration paid to Granny Kempoch was so great that when it was said of Mary Lamont that she intended to throw the great stone into the sea, a hefty feat for a young woman, the utmost consternation was felt by the good people of Gourock. In their opinion the danger to shipping would be great and wrecks would be innumerable. It seems that in 1622 the information to hand concerning the navigation of the channel must have been very scanty. Even if a stone six feet high were cast into the sea it would make little difference to shipping then and in these days still less.

However, Mary Lamont, was regarded as a witch, and so to avoid any possible complications she was burnt alive. The same motives inspired

LOCH LONG

DONALD MAXWELL

the good Protestants of Gourock as inspired Queen Mary at Smithfield—fear of something beyond argument or reason. To allow either a witch or a heretic to survive might bring down the vengeance of heaven upon the whole community. Most cruelty can be traced to fear.

Gourock is beautiful, especially from a distance, when the promontory crowned by its shapely church tower can be seen against the mountain distance across the shining water. It is the first place on the Clyde on this bank where industry gives place to purely scenic delights. The clang of the yard is left behind, and yachts appear, in the winter their hulls looming up, making a strange foreground on the eastern side of the town, and in summer making butterfly beauty up and down the locks.

To take stock of this mouth of the Clyde, for I suppose where the Clyde runs into the Firth is the mouth, I climbed high up on the moor overlooking the town, and thence could see great waters spread out in all their distant beauty, thrusting silvery arms into the hollows of the hills

I could look back towards Greenock, that grey town

> " That pipes the morning up before the lark
> With shrieking steam, and from a hundred stacks
> Lacquers the sooty sky ; where hammers clang
> On iron hulls, and cranes in harbours creak,
> Rattle and swing, whole cargoes on their necks ;
> Where men sweat gold that others hoard or spend,
> And lurk like vermin in their narrow streets." [1]

[1] John Davidson.

Or, looking the other way and across the Firth we
see a strand

> " Spangled with hamlets, and the wooded steeps,
> Whose rocky tops behind each other press,
> Fantastically carved like antique helms
> High-hung in heaven's cloudy armoury." [1]

Or, turning my gaze south, with a little geographical
license I could almost gaze upon distant Rothesay
down across the Firth.

> " It's a bonnie boy i' the mornin',
> An' bonnier at the noon :
> But bonniest when the sun draps
> An' red comes up the moon ;
> When the mist creeps ower the Cumbraes
> An' Arran peaks are grey,
> An' the great black hills like sleepin' kings,
> Set grand roun' Rothesay Bay." [2]

The weather was clear and I could see a long way,
lights and shadows chased each other across the
heights, and a town, now dark, would suddenly
lighten, and a sunny hill-side would seem to frown
at times and rear itself grimly into the sky.

The lights and shadows playing on the peaks far
north make me think of Turner's *Liber Studiorum*
plate, "Ben Arthur"; and the glamour of this
" romantic landscape " brings to mind the visit of
Wordsworth and his sister and Coleridge and Rogers.

[1] John Davidson. [2] Mrs. Craik.

HOLY LOCH

The strange melancholy of it all seems to impress the Wordsworths, or else they were suffering from a fit of the " blues." " The stillness of the mountains," writes Dorothy Wordsworth, " the motion of the waves, the streaming torrents, the sea-birds, the fishing boats were all melancholy ; yet still, occupied as my mind was with other things, I thought of the long windings through which the waters of this sea had come to this inland retreat, visiting the inner solitudes of the mountains, and I could have wished to have mused out a summer's day on the shores of the lake."

Rogers has left some lines describing Loch Long which show a deeper insight into the landscape of this gorge :

> " Upon another shore I stood
> And looked upon another flood :
> Old Ocean's self ('tis he who fills
> That vast and awful depth of hills)."

The waters of Gareloch lie hidden from here, but the peaks by Gareloch Head disclose their track. It is in the shadow of these crags, by the Fruin Burn that Alasdair Macgregor fell upon the Colquhouns and killed one hundred and forty of them, burning down their farm buildings and pillaging their land. This was the last straw to the patience of all neighbouring clans. The Government of Scotland (1603) made it a capital offence to bear the name of Macgregor. Alasdair was captured and hanged in Edinburgh. The attempt to exterminate the clan went on for generations, and the outlaws took other names to evade the consequences of the ban.

It seems that some of them, to add insult to injury, took the name of Colquhoun. I am not, as you can see, very well up in Scottish history, and I may be wrong, but I had a strange confirmation of this changing of names only the other day. I was told of an elderly lady in Helensburgh who, on hearing a certain family referred to as Colquhouns, cried out :

" Colquhouns ! They're naught but dirty Macgregors."

It was a striking instance of the fact that the old clan feeling is not entirely dead in Scotland.

THE CLOCH

TWILIGHT NEAR INVERKIP

THE COASTWISE LIGHTS

HOLY Loch is said to have been given this name because a ship laden with earth from Palestine was wrecked there. This ship, in consequence of directions being given by St. Mungo that holy ground should be laid upon the site of Glasgow's Cathedral, was bearing its precious freight up the Firth of Clyde when a sudden storm arose and she was driven into the shore at Kilmun, and the earth scattered upon the shore. Thus, having a consecrated site, it was necessary and pious to build a church upon it, and that, so old legend tells us, is how the Church of Kilmun came to be there.

Another and more probable origin of the name Holy Loch is the fact that a monastery was built there in the sixth century. As every one who writes about this loch has a different theory as to the origin of its name, I do not see why I should not hazard a guess as well. If the mountain known as Bishop's Seat was so called in olden time, may it be that the waters which lay at the bishop's feet were considered holy, in an age when the Scot had not quite so violent a prejudice against bishops !

A much-travelled Scot being asked one day what he considered the best stretch of landscape in the world replied that it was the walk from Gourock to the Cloch Lighthouse. Unfortunately his interrogator had never been to Scotland and was therefore unable to appreciate the justice of the verdict. So he tried his friend again.

" But supposing," he said, " that we leave out the walk from Gourock to the Cloch Lighthouse, what would you consider was the next best walk ? " Without a moment's hesitation the loyal man of the Clyde gave the inevitable reply :

" Why, then, it would be the walk from the Cloch Lighthouse to Gourock."

History does not relate whether or not his friend pushed him in the river or did anything drastic. I suppose any change from this conservative loyalty

DONALD MAXWELL

THE RIVIERA OF SCOTLAND

would have made the British Empire what it isn't. However, it is a good story, and I affirm, having travelled half the world over in search of views, that there is something in the opinion. Few coasts can show such a piece of road as the road from Gourock to the Cloch.

The nearest thing in my mind, if you can forget the fact that it sometimes rains in Scotland, is the lower Corniche Road in the Riviera. There is a distinct similarity in the stony shore, the overhanging of trees, and the glimpses of heights above. In one thing, however, the Scottish Riviera can give points to the South of France—it has another shore, a land of blue peaks and green banks—the Riviera looking out upon the Alps, with the sea-road of many nations in between ; at Gourock you can combine the joys of living at the South Foreland, the coast of Monaco, and the Italian lakes all at once—that is, if the weather is fine.

Inverkip lies round the corner towards Wemyss Bay, and might be described as the first place on the Firth of Clyde, as far as this side is concerned. The measured mile, well known to all marine engineers, is marked upon this shore, and all Clyde-built ships do their steam trials up and down this part of the Firth.

Rothesay and Hunter's Quay are beloved of yachtsmen in the summer. The steam yacht, that innovation at first stoutly resisted by the yacht clubs, won its way to favour in these waters. At first the Royal Yacht Squadron regarded with grave disapproval any one who so much as *looked* at a yacht that travelled by mechanical power. A ban of excommunication was solemnly passed on any member who bought or built a steam yacht. The engineers of the Clyde, however, soon caused this prejudice to die down.

The Islands of Bute and Arran lie outside the scope of this record, but we feel in all this part some hope and anticipation of them as the broad waters spread out to join with the sea.

Hear Wordsworth's sentiments:

> " Arran ! a single-crested Teneriffe,
> A St. Helena next—in shape and hue,
> Varying her crowded peaks and ridges blue :
> Who but must covet a cloud-seat, or skiff
> Built for the air, or winged Hippogriff ?
> That he might fly, where no one could pursue,
> From this dull Monster and her sooty crew ; [1]
> And, as a God, light on the topmost cliff,
> Impotent wish ! which reason would despise . . ."

It would be interesting to know what the poet would have written had he been able to leave the dull Monster in a seaplane and circle round the topmost cliff at two hundred and fifty miles an hour !

The difference between the two sides of the Firth of Clyde is very striking. Both Gourock and Dunoon are flourishing seaside places, but the road

[1] This last is an allusion to the steam-boat on which Wordsworth was writing.

LOOKING ACROSS TO DUNOON

from Gourock leads on to lonely shores and to a coast still wild and primitive in many long stretches, while the waterside for miles and miles near Dunoon is almost suburban in its villadom. Some of it might be at Surbiton with the Thames enormously enlarged.

It is for this reason that during the summer I prefer the Renfrew shore. In spite of its accessibility to Glasgow it is the less exploited shore, and I think has far finer views. From the Dunoon side the Renfrew coast is comparatively tame. Even the rugged heights around Holy Loch seem grander from a distance. At Dunoon the observer has too much foreground to negotiate. From across the water, however, the high peaks of the distance make a magnificent sky-line of broken outline.

On page 169 I have endeavoured to render one of those twilight effects when the evening light of the broken sky in the north-west still lingered in hills. The solemn background of jagged peaks contrasted with this fringe of watering-places at their feet—a long line of many lamps. One belated yacht was visible, creeping against a failing tide. In the foreground, some meadowland and rows of haycocks gave a domestic touch to a landscape that otherwise might have become too sombre.

Especially at sunset or at twilight is this romantic landscape to be seen at its best. When the last light has died down in the fiery north-west and the myriad lights of the Cowan shore make strange constellations along the beaches, casting many a reflection into the glittering waters, there comes a wonderful stillness into the air. Through tree-trunks and foliage varied glimpses of the magic landscape can be seen by the motorist or the pedestrian as he returns toward Gourock, and then, if the tide be in flood, he will find, travelling the same way, the homeward-bound ships of Glasgow, a moving galaxy of white lights and green.

From the ends of the earth have they come, and many a Clydesdale "Mac" pops up his head from the engine-room below, to breathe once more the caller air of home.

THE COAST ROAD BY THE CLOCH

BY THE SAME AUTHOR

UNKNOWN SOMERSET

Illustrated in Colour and Line by the Author.
Foolscap 4to.   15s. net.

UNKNOWN DORSET

Illustrated in Colour and Line by the Author.
Foolscap 4to.   15s. net

" Perhaps the highest tribute one can pay to ' Unknown Dorset ' is to say that
it is just as good as ' Unknown Sussex ' and ' Unknown Kent '—exquisite books
which every explorer, whether on foot or awheel, should possess.   How well Mr.
Maxwell writes, and how rarely provocative are his line and colour illustrations."
—*Spectator.*

UNKNOWN NORFOLK

Illustrated in Colour and Black and White by the Author.
Foolscap 4to.   15s. net.

" The letterpress is written with pleasant humour in gossipy style and beautifully
printed.   Mr. Maxwell has illuminated his search of the picturesque with brush
and pen, in colour and black and white."—*Times Literary Supplement.*

UNKNOWN SUFFOLK

With 20 Illustrations in Colour and many in Line by the Author.
Foolscap 4to.   15s. net.

" When I read Mr. Donald Maxwell's delightful new book ' Unknown Suffolk '
I had an almost irresistible longing to follow in his footsteps then and there.   What
a charming writer he is, and what an exquisite artist !   Mr. Maxwell is, in my
opinion, the ideal explorer.   ' Unknown Suffolk ' takes its rightful place beside
Mr. Maxwell's ' Unknown ' of Kent, Surrey, Sussex, Essex, and Norfolk, of their
kind as near perfection as not to matter in the very least."—*Tatler* (Richard King.)

JOHN LANE THE BODLEY HEAD LTD., VIGO ST., W. 1

UNKNOWN ESSEX

With 30 Illustrations in Colour and 95 in Line by the Author.
Foolscap 4to. 15s. net.

" Mr. Maxwell has had exceptional opportunities for making acquaintance with some of the tidal waters, and he has learnt the fascinations of the grey and lonely marches through which they wind. His accounts of his rambles form a pleasant setting to his many attractive sketches in colour and in line."—*Times Literary Supplement.*

UNKNOWN KENT

Illustrated in Colour and in Black and White by the Author.
Second Edition. Foolscap 4to. 12s. 6d. net.

" Mr. Donald Maxwell's inspiring and beautiful new book perfectly produced at The Bodley Head. It captures the *genius loci* of the country as cunningly as Kinglake captured the desert in ' Eothen '. Mr. Maxwell is not only an artist in paint and pencil—his sketches are a sheer delight—but he is an artist in words as well, who can see into the very heart of things."—*Graphic.*

UNKNOWN SUSSEX

Illustrated in Colour and Black and White by the Author.
Third Edition. Foolscap 4to. 15s. net.

" This book gives refreshing peeps into the rolling downs and nooks and crannies of one of our most lovely counties. Mr. Maxwell has the double gift of graphic and humorous description in words, as well as of original and delightful portrayal in colour and monochrome."—*Daily Express.*

" This is a book I should like to give to all men of Sussex to remind them, and to all foreigners to inform them, of the fair plot of ground which we of the South have the privilege to inherit."—*Daily Graphic.*

UNKNOWN SURREY

Illustrated in Colour and Black and White by the Author.
Foolscap 4to. 15s. net.

" Mr. Maxwell has succeeded in writing a very pleasant book ; and his pictures are delightful."—*Times Literary Supplement.*

" ' Unknown Surrey ' is the best of the series. It is a book to make the man in search of a holiday decide to go into the heart of Surrey and lose himself."—*Westminster Gazette.*

JOHN LANE THE BODLEY HEAD LTD., VIGO ST., W.1